Visit the Corinthian Church Again

Visit the Corinthian Church Again

An Exegetical Commentary of Paul's Second Epistle to the Corinthians

Bob Koonce Th. D.

Visit the Corinthian Church Again
An Exegetical Commentary on Paul's Second Epistle to the Corinthians

Bob Koonce Bible Commentaries Book Two

Copyright © 2019 Bob Koonce/John Koonce

All rights reserved. Please do not reproduce in any manner or form, or store in any type retrieval system without prior express written consent by the copywrite holders. Brief quotations may be used in the event of a literary review

Unless otherwise identified, all scripture used are taken from the Authorized King James Version

ISBN-13: 9781074761257
Independently published

Nonfiction > Religion > Biblical Commentary > New Testament
Nonfiction > Religion > Biblical Studies > Paul's Letters

Printed in the United States of America

Introduction

'Visit the Corinthian Church Again; An Exegetical Commentary of Paul's Second Epistle to the Corinthians,' is a follow up commentary, in the Bob Koonce Bible Commentary Series; Visit the Corinthian Church.

This work follows the same formula the popular I Corinthian commentary uses. Each chapter in this work starts with the corresponding scripture chapter in II Corinthians. Then verse by verse, Bishop Bob Koonce lays out his expertise, sharing his years of studying, praying and teaching, explaining them with easy to read and understandable language.

Although this is an exegetical commentary, the word study is easy to follow and understand.

Bishop Koonce pastored several churches before he moved to Gibson City. He started the church there in 1963 until he retired as Pastor in 1994 and was elevated to the title of Bishop the same year. His insight during his teaching sessions brought him into the national spotlight. His teachings on prophecy afforded him the opportunities to travel and share his views on that subject. Bishop Koonce was a scholar in other areas beside prophecy; such as the books of Romans, The Corinthians and Old Testament studies such as Noah's Ark and the Tabernacle in the Wilderness.

Take the journey with Bob Koonce through this commentary. You will find the trip rewarding.

Other Books by the Bob Koonce

Visit the Corinthian Church; An Exegetical Commentary of Paul's First Epistle to the Corinthians.

Understanding Revelation; The Revelation of Jesus Christ, a commentary

The Name Above Every Name; A Study of the Tetragrammaton

The Heavens Declare His Glory; Poetry and Prose

Everyday Help for Everyday Christian; 13 Bible Study Lessons

Walk With Me Through the Word; 13 Bible Study Lessons

Beyond This Hill: A Novel

The Man Called Peter-Commentary on 1st and 2nd Peter

Table of Content

Table of Contents

Visit the Corinthian Church Again	i
Visit the Corinthian Church Again	iii
Introduction	v
Other Books by the Bob Koonce	vi
Table of Content	vii
CHAPTER ONE	1
CHAPTER TWO	13
CHAPTER THREE	25
CHAPTER FOUR	33
CHAPTER FIVE	43
CHAPTER SIX	55
CHAPTER SEVEN	65
CHAPTER EIGHT	73
CHAPTER NINE	83
CHAPTER TEN	89
CHAPTER ELEVEN	99
CHAPTER TWELVE	115
CHAPTER THIRTEEN	129

I've been privileged to have known Bishop Bob Koonce for most of my memorable life. There are few men that can keep you focused on relevant Biblical topics as he can, and even fewer men who can keep you enthused. Bishop Koonce has a unique way of bringing some of the most important revelations to light in way that anyone can understand them. His commentaries are some of the most information packed yet understandable commentaries that I have ever had the privilege of reading. Bishop Bob Koonce has a gift to share with the world, and that is the gift of knowledge.

Michael Weedman
Pastor, The Pentecostals of Sparta
Sparta TN. 38583

This great commentary on the book of I Corinthians is a Godsend to the students of Biblical Apostolic University. From the time that Bishop Koonce gave permission for me to use it as part of the BAU curriculum, it has been a tremendous blessing to students and student-pastors.

One pastor emailed me, saying that I Corinthians was full of great insights and helped him understand some very difficult questions concerning this book. After this pastor had completed his studies, the opportunity presented itself for him to teach the material he had just studied. His church was blessed by the wisdom of Bishop Koonce through his explanations of the scripture and showing its application in their lives, both ministers and saints alike.

BAU has never had one complaint or serious question from any student concerning the commentary and enlightened insight Bishop Koonce displayed in this book.

I strongly suggest that every pastor .... and potential pastor/teacher buy this book and study it. Do not just read it .... study it. There is great wisdom and understanding in the pages of this commentary on Paul's first letter to the Corinthian church.

Dr. Billy D. Bates, Th. D.
PRESIDENT - BAU

CHAPTER ONE

1 Paul, an apostle of Jesus Christ by the will of God, and Timothy our brother, unto the church of God which is at Corinth, with all the saints which are in all Achaia:

2 Grace be to you and peace from God our Father, and from the Lord Jesus Christ.

3 Blessed be God, even the Father of our Lord Jesus Christ, the Father of mercies, and the God of all comfort;

4 Who comforteth us in all our tribulation, that we may be able to comfort them which are in any trouble, by the comfort wherewith we ourselves are comforted of God.

5 For as the sufferings of Christ abound in us, so our consolation also aboundeth by Christ.

6 And whether we be afflicted, it is for your consolation and salvation, which is effectual in the enduring of the same sufferings which we also suffer: or whether we be comforted, it is for your consolation and salvation.

7 And our hope of you is stedfast, knowing, that as ye are partakers of the sufferings, so shall ye be also of the consolation.

8 For we would not, brethren, have you ignorant of our trouble which came to us in Asia, that we were pressed out of measure, above strength, insomuch that we despaired even of life:

9 But we had the sentence of death in ourselves, that we should not trust in ourselves, but in God which raiseth the dead:

10 Who delivered us from so great a death, and doth deliver: in whom we trust that he will yet deliver us;

11 Ye also helping together by prayer for us, that for the gift bestowed upon us by the means of many persons thanks may be given by many on our behalf.

12 For our rejoicing is this, the testimony of our conscience, that in simplicity and godly sincerity, not with fleshly wisdom, but by the grace of God, we have had our conversation in the world, and more abundantly to you-ward.

13 For we write none other things unto you, than what ye read or acknowledge; and I trust ye shall acknowledge even to the end;

14 As also ye have acknowledged us in part, that we are your rejoicing, even as ye also are ours in the day of the Lord Jesus.

15 And in this confidence, I was minded to come unto you before, that ye might have a second benefit;

16 And to pass by you into Macedonia, and to come again out of Macedonia unto you, and of you to be brought on my way toward Judaea.

17 When I therefore was thus minded, did I use lightness? or the things that I purpose, do I purpose according to the flesh, that with me there should be yea yea, and nay nay?

18 But as God is true, our word toward you was not yea and nay.

9 For the Son of God, Jesus Christ, who was preached among you by us, even by me and Silvanus and Timotheus, was not yea and nay, but in him was yea.

20 For all the promises of God in him are yea, and in him Amen, unto the glory of God by us.

21 Now he which stablisheth us with you in Christ, and hath anointed us, is God;

22 Who hath also sealed us, and given the earnest of the Spirit in our hearts.

23 Moreover I call God for a record upon my soul, that to spare you I came not as yet unto Corinth.

24 Not for that we have dominion over your faith, but are helpers of your joy: for by faith ye stand.

Verse 1:
Paul, an apostle of Jesus Christ by the will of God, and Timothy our brother, unto the church of God which is at Corinth, with all the saints which are in all Achaia:

Timothy apparently was with Paul when the Apostle wrote the second epistle to the Corinthian church. Much speculation about a time period in which this epistle was sent has been set forth, but no clear evidence has been given to positively establish a time.

Corinth was located strategically near the center of the northern portion of the Roman Empire. Corinth, once destroyed, was restored during the reign of Julius Caesar. It was a young commercial city, filled with wickedness and idolatry. Its people, though primarily Gentile, was composed of numerous Jews also.

En holēi tēi Achaiāi – "in all Achaia." The Romans divided Greece into two provinces (Achaia and Macedonia). Macedonia included Illyricum, Epirus, and Thessaly. Achaia, both Attica and the Peloponnesus, was all of Greece southward. The restored Corinth was made the capital of Achaia where the pro-consul resided. Paul didn't mention other churches in Achaia other than using the word, "saints."

Athens was in Achaia, but it is not clear that there was a church there at that time. According to Acts 17:34, some converts had been won in that area. There was a church in Cenchreae, the eastern port of Corinth (Romans 16:1). Paul used two names, Achaia and Macedonia, together in I Corinthians 9:2. His words seem to imply that he included the whole of Achaia, and not merely the area in and about the city of Corinth. The Greek word, *holēi*, translates all.

...unto the church of God which is at Corinth (verse 1). This salutation speaks volumes if this epistle does indeed follow the First Corinthians epistle. Considering the many rebukes from Paul to the Corinthian church in First Corinthians, verse 1 of this chapter still proclaims, "...church of God...at Corinth." Despite the false doctrines, the schisms, and the power struggles in that church, the congregation must have heeded Paul's instructions.

Verses 2:
Grace be to you and peace from God our Father, and from the Lord Jesus Christ.

This verse does not embrace the assumption that there is more than one Person in the Godhead. *To wit, that God was in Christ, reconciling the world unto himself, not imputing their trespasses unto them; and hath committed unto us the word of reconciliation* (2Corinthians 5:19).

To accept a Trinity of God is to accept 2 Spirits in the Godhead; (Spirit of God + a Holy Spirit, making 2 Spirits).

Verses 3-4:
3 Blessed be God, even the Father of our Lord Jesus Christ, the Father of mercies, and the God of all comfort;

4 Who comforteth us in all our tribulation, that we may be able to comfort them which are in any trouble, by the comfort wherewith we ourselves are comforted of God.

Jesus left His disciples with a promise of a Comforter (John 16:7). *Nevertheless I tell you the truth; It is expedient for you that I go away: for if I go not away, the Comforter will not come unto you; but if I depart, I will send him unto you.* And, verse 4: W*ho comforteth us in all our tribulation, that we may be able to comfort them which are in any trouble, by the comfort wherewith we ourselves are comforted of God.*

In John 14:18, Jesus said, "*I will not leave you comfortless: I will come to you.*"

Verse 5:
For as the sufferings of Christ abound in us, so our consolation also aboundeth by Christ.

Clearly our consolation is provided by Jesus Christ and made possible by His own agony unto death on a cross. *But he was wounded for our transgressions, he was bruised for our iniquities: the chastisement of our peace was upon him; and with his stripes we are healed* (Isaiah 53:5).

A Christian will never go anywhere Jesus has not already been; be tempted with anything that He has not already faced and overcome; or suffer anything that Jesus did not face. He has already triumphed over every imaginable thing that the devil has concocted. He is the Comforter!

6 And whether we be afflicted, it is for your consolation and salvation, which is effectual in the enduring of the same sufferings which we also suffer: or whether we be comforted, it is for your consolation and salvation.

And whether we be afflicted... Better stated, perhaps, this expression would insert "when" for "whether." The Apostle was well acquainted with afflictions, having already been stoned, beaten unmercifully at Philippi, and fled for his life more than once.

Afflicted in this verse surely must define *physical* abuse, especially in view of his using the word "sufferings" in the next verse.

...it is for your consolation and salvation. How so? Paul explained by adding, *"is effectual in the enduring of the same sufferings".* 2 Timothy 3:12 adds these words: *Yea, and all that will live godly in Christ Jesus shall suffer persecution.*

...or whether we be comforted, it is for your consolation and salvation. Paul shifted the focus back onto himself and those with him. A paraphrase of this verse would read, "When we receive peace, we remain stronger in mind and spirit to serve you. And by your witnessing the power of God in us, you take hope in your own afflictions. That hope will result in your own salvation."

7 And our hope of you is stedfast, knowing, that as ye are partakers of the sufferings, so shall ye be also of the consolation.

Paul did not address every person that concluded himself to be a member of the church at Corinth. He wrote to the "members of the Body of Christ" in that congregation. In his first epistle to that church, he addressed the many problems there. In verse 7 here, he spoke to the faithful persons in that church that had stood steadfastly for Christ.

And our hope of you is stedfast, knowing... "You are suffering the same things that we are suffering, SO, you will experience the same consolation that we receive!" (Paraphrase)

8 For we would not, brethren, have you ignorant of our trouble which came to us in Asia, that we were pressed out of measure, above strength, insomuch that we despaired even of life:

Of the several Bible commentaries I resorted to concerning this verse, I found the same answer. They all state that the trouble to which Paul referred in this verse, is not known. There is no mention in any other of his epistles where he used the words, *"pressed out of measure, above strength, insomuch that we despaired even of life."*

It is my opinion that Paul may have been captured, sentenced to die, and tortured often until he fainted from the torture. Those with him would have suffered the same sentence and abuse. I do not think that this verse relates to any of the places mentioned in the Book of Acts. There is no record of the names of any of the churches in the region then known as Asia, the upper portion of present-day Turkey. Paul wrote from prison that all the churches in Asia had turned against him.

In support of my opinion, I include a Scripture found in Acts 16:6: *Now when they had gone throughout Phrygia and the region of Galatia, and were forbidden of the Holy Ghost to preach the word in Asia.* Scripture records Paul leaving Ephesus, then going into Macedonia. From Philippi (in Macedonia), he eventually went to Athens and to Corinth. Other than the churches mentioned in Achaia, Macedonia, and the city of Ephesus, there is no mention of any church in the region than known as Asia.

I believe the information I've given in the 2 preceding paragraphs, gives strong evidence that Paul's words, *"our trouble which came to us in Asia",* surely must describe a region, not identified by name in Scripture.

9 But we had the sentence of death in ourselves, that we should not trust in ourselves, but in God which raiseth the dead:

I agree with this comment from the Clarke's Commentary on this verse:

"We had the sentence of death in ourselves - The tribulation was so violent and overwhelming, that he had no hope of escaping death."

With reservation, I agree with Clarke and other commentators on this opinion for this verse. I do not believe that this interpretation is applicable to the preceding verse 8, however. In that verse, I state that I believe it possible that Paul and company faced death sentences and related torture while awaiting their executions.

10 Who delivered us from so great a death, and doth deliver: in whom we trust that he will yet deliver us;

Who delivered us from so great a death... This expression may be interpreted in 2 ways. The words, *so great a death*, could be understood to apply to an eternal death in hell. They also may be saying that Paul had been delivered from a horrendous physical death. Paul continued by writing, *doth deliver* (present), and, *he will yet deliver us;* (future delivering).

11 Ye also helping together by prayer for us, that for the gift bestowed upon us by the means of many persons thanks may be given by many on our behalf.

Rightly, Scripture affirms that multiple people agreeing for a cause and praying for that cause, brings results. *Again I say unto you, That if two of you shall agree on earth as touching anything that they shall ask, it shall be done for them of my Father which is in heaven* (Matthew 18:19).

Paul gave thanks for the help he received from the many people that had and were praying for him.

John Wesley explained this verse in these few, simple words:
"You likewise - As well as other churches. Helping with us by prayer, that for the gift - Namely, my deliverance. Bestowed upon us by means of many persons - Praying for it, thanks may be given by many."

12 For our rejoicing is this, the testimony of our conscience, that in simplicity and godly sincerity, not with fleshly wisdom, but by the grace of God, we have had our conversation in the world, and more abundantly to you-ward.

I translate this verse thus: "My conscience affirms that we have not flaunted our education in our preaching and teaching. It is God's grace by which we were able to convert you to God. And we have ministered more to you than to other Gentiles."

13 For we write none other things unto you, than what ye read or acknowledge; and I trust ye shall acknowledge even to the end;

I believe that the word, *acknowledge* (present tense), and used twice in this sentence, should be *acknowledged (*past tense) I paraphrase this verse as: "We're not writing new things, only the things you have previously acknowledged, and I trust you will not fail them to the day of your death."

14 As also ye have acknowledged us in part, that we are your rejoicing, even as ye also are ours in the day of the Lord Jesus.

As also ye have acknowledged us in part... I paraphrase this verse thus: *"*Some of you have accepted us, some of you haven't. Because of your conversion by our preaching, you can now rejoice. And because you heard and repented, we now rejoice. All this will be so important when the Lord Jesus comes for His bride."

Clarke's Commentary renders the following on this verse:
"Have acknowledged us in part - Απο μερους may signify here not in part, but some of you; and it is evident, from the distracted state of the Corinthians, and the opposition raised there against the apostle, that it was only a part of them that did acknowledge him, and receive and profit by his epistles and advice."

15 And in this confidence, I was minded to come unto you before, that ye might have a second benefit;
16 And to pass by you into Macedonia, and to come again out of Macedonia unto you, and of you to be brought on my way toward Judaea.

In First Corinthians 16:5-7, Paul wrote that it was his intention to visit Corinth a second time.
5 Now I will come unto you, when I shall pass through Macedonia: for I do pass through Macedonia.
6 And it may be that I will abide, yea, and winter with you, that ye may bring me on my journey whithersoever I go.
7 For I will not see you now by the way; but I trust to tarry a while with you, if the Lord permit.

It appears that his intention to visit Corinth at that particular time was the "second benefit" of which he earlier wrote. But, somewhat strangely, Paul seems to have turned abruptly to again defend his apostleship.

17 When I therefore was thus minded, did I use lightness? or the things that I purpose, do I purpose according to the flesh, that with me there should be yea yea, and nay nay?

It must be remembered that there were some in the Corinthian congregation that resented Paul. It appears that the dissenters in the church were then accusing him of changing his mind about visiting Corinth. The yea, yea, nay, nay expressions have the connotation of affirmation of something and then a denial of the same. The dissenters in the church were evidently saying that Paul was prone to changing his mind without reason. It is reasonable to think that the dissenters might have used expressions much like the following sentences. "He changes his mind all the time. You can't depend on what he says!"

Matthew Henry lends the following on this passage:
"The apostle here vindicates himself from the imputation of levity and inconstancy, in that he did not hold his purpose of coming to them at Corinth. His adversaries there sought all occasions to blemish his character, and reflect upon his conduct; and, it seemed, they took hold of this handle to reproach his person and discredit his ministry."

Barnes' N.T. Notes gives this explanation:
"Did I use lightness? The word ἐλαφρια elaphria (from ἐλαφρός elaphros) means properly lightness in weight. Here it is used in reference to the mind; and in a sense similar to our word levity, as denoting lightness of temper or conduct; inconstancy, changeableness, or fickleness. This charge had been probably made that he had made the promise without any due consideration, or without any real purpose of performing, it; or that he had made it in a trifling and thoughtless manner. By the interrogative form here, he sharply denies that it was a purpose formed in a light and trifling manner."

18 But as God is true, our word toward you was not yea and nay.

But as God is true... What greater witness than God? Paul banked his defense of his preaching as being affirmative, unwavering, and truthful as God Himself is true. God never changes, thus, Paul defended himself by using God as Witness to the fact that he was not double-minded.

19 For the Son of God, Jesus Christ, who was preached among you by us, even by me and Silvanus and Timotheus, was not yea and nay, but in him was yea.
20 For all the promises of God in him are yea, and in him Amen, unto the glory of God by us.

Paul lashed out at the dissenters in the Corinthian church: "There was no yes, then no, or maybe and then maybe not; our message to you was *the Son of God, Jesus Christ... For all the promises of God in him are yea, and in him Amen.*

Malachi 3:6 states: *For I am the LORD, I change not;*

21 Now he which stablisheth us with you in Christ, and hath anointed us, is God;
22 Who hath also sealed us, and given the earnest of the Spirit in our hearts.

Established, anointed, and sealed by God. One God Who bestows so much upon the ministry.

...and given the earnest of the Spirit in our hearts—a gift in advance—the Holy Ghost baptism.

23 Moreover I call God for a record upon my soul, that to spare you I came not as yet unto Corinth.

At face value, the words, *to spare you*, sound like a threat. The words may have been intended to infer discipline, yet the words may also carry the connotation that Paul spoke of the physical burden his presence there would cause them. Guests were housed in homes, sometimes for extended periods of times. By not going to Corinth at that time, he *spared* them.

24 Not for that we have dominion over your faith, but are helpers of your joy: for by faith ye stand.

Hebrews 13:17 speaks of the authority of Christian ministry:

Obey them that have the rule over you, and submit yourselves: for they watch for your souls, as they that must give account, that they may do it with joy, and not with grief: for that is unprofitable for you.

It is generally believed that Paul authored the Book of Hebrews. If that be true, the Apostle would naturally have known that verse. Whether he was the author, though, really is of no great importance. He had exercised his authority throughout the whole epistle of First Corinthians.

In verse 24, he spoke as a father, not as a ruler. Despite the obstinacy of the dissenters in that church, Paul demonstrated his love for them. *but are helpers of your joy: for by faith ye stand.*

Bob Koonce Th. D.

CHAPTER TWO

1 But I determined this with myself, that I would not come again to you in heaviness.

2 For if I make you sorry, who is he then that maketh me glad, but the same which is made sorry by me?

3 And I wrote this same unto you, lest, when I came, I should have sorrow from them of whom I ought to rejoice; having confidence in you all, that my joy is the joy of you all.

4 For out of much affliction and anguish of heart I wrote unto you with many tears; not that ye should be grieved, but that ye might know the love which I have more abundantly unto you.

5 But if any have caused grief, he hath not grieved me, but in part: that I may not overcharge you all.

6 Sufficient to such a man is this punishment, which was inflicted of many.

7 So that contrariwise ye ought rather to forgive him, and comfort him, lest perhaps such a one should be swallowed up with overmuch sorrow.

8 Wherefore I beseech you that ye would confirm your love toward him.

9 For to this end also did I write, that I might know the proof of you, whether ye be obedient in all things.

10 To whom ye forgive any thing, I forgive also: for if I forgave any thing, to whom I forgave it, for your sakes forgave I it in the person of Christ;

11 Lest Satan should get an advantage of us: for we are not ignorant of his devices.

12 Furthermore, when I came to Troas to preach Christ's gospel, and a door was opened unto me of the Lord,

13 I had no rest in my spirit, because I found not Titus my brother: but taking my leave of them, I went from thence into Macedonia.

14 Now thanks be unto God, which always causeth us to triumph in Christ, and maketh manifest the savour of his knowledge by us in every place.

15 For we are unto God a sweet savour of Christ, in them that are saved, and in them that perish:
16 To the one we are the savour of death unto death; and to the other the savour of life unto life. And who is sufficient for these things?
17 For we are not as many, which corrupt the word of God: but as of sincerity, but as of God, in the sight of God speak we in Christ.

This chapter is another example of human error. Chapter 1 did not end with its last verse. The subject matter of the last several verses of that chapter is continued through verse 4 of this chapter. Well-intentioned scholars certainly made unintended mistakes in their divisions of chapters and verses of the Bible.

The Bible was fist divided into chapters, then later into verses. Since the early 13th century, most copies and editions of the Bible, except the shortest Books, were divided into divisions (chapters). Since the mid-16th century, editors further subdivided each chapter into verses -- each consisting of a few short lines or sentences. Sometimes a sentence spans more than one verse, and sometimes there is more than one sentence in a single verse.

The first Bible in English to use both chapters and verses is the Geneva Bible, published in 1560. These verse divisions soon gained acceptance as a standard way to notate verses, and have since been used in nearly all English Bibles, and the vast majority of those in other languages. Though the Bible is inerrant, copiers of the thousands of ancient manuscripts did contain errors. For that reason alone, Scripture must be confirmed by Scripture. A single Scripture does not constitute a Bible truth. Matthew 18:13 and Second Corinthians 13:1 tell us that *"in the mouth of 2 or 3 witnesses every word is established."*

1 But I determined this with myself, that I would not come again to you in heaviness.

But I determined this with myself, that I would not come again to you in heaviness in v*erse 1,* connects directly with verse 23 of the first chapter: *Moreover I call God for a record upon my soul, that to spare you I came not as yet unto Corinth,* Though Paul's first epistle to the Corinthians was laced with reprimands, he strove to portray his immense love throughout that epistle. Here in verse 1 of this chapter, he wrote, *not come again to you in heaviness*. How greatly did his love shine forth!

2 For if I make you sorry, who is he then that maketh me glad, but the same which is made sorry by me?

This verse might be better understood as: *You who have made me happy are those that I made sorry.*

3 And I wrote this same unto you, lest, when I came, I should have sorrow from them of whom I ought to rejoice; having confidence in you all, that my joy is the joy of you all.

Being the apostle to the Gentiles, Paul faced dangerous situations in every city he preached. While the other apostles preached largely to Jews, Paul preached to Gentiles. He was like a lighted match dropped onto dry grass. He preached and won souls everywhere he went. A Gentile church was evidence of his willingness to die for Jesus Christ. Having jeopardized his own life for every Gentile church and then see corruptness within a congregation, helps us understand his heartbreak and tears. Great was his love for souls.

"I scolded you in my first epistle, hoping that you would correct your faults. At my coming again, I would be sorrowful had you not obeyed my advice. I would be disappointed in you when it is you who should cause me to rejoice." (paraphrase)

Clarke's Commentary suggests the following on this verse:
"And I wrote this same unto you - This I particularly marked in my first epistle to you; earnestly desiring your reformation, lest, if I came before this had taken place, I must have come with a rod, and have inflicted punishment on the transgressors."

Several commentaries indicate they believe that Paul referred to the incestuous affair that he addressed in I Corinthians. Greater certainty of the accuracy of that contention could be made if it were possible to positively determine that II Corinthians was indeed Paul's second epistle to the Corinthians. Verse 14 of this chapter reads: *Behold, the third time I am ready to come to you;* We are led to wonder whether he here spoke of an epistle or a physical visit.

4 For out of much affliction and anguish of heart I wrote unto you with many tears; not that ye should be grieved, but that ye might know the love which I have more abundantly unto you.

For out of much affliction and anguish of heart I <u>wrote</u>... Paul described his reason for writing. Rather than write a lengthy explanation for my opinion on this verse, I refer the reader to the first paragraph following verse 3 of this chapter. Clearly Paul wept much and groaned in his spirit over the problem here addressed. So much like a father weeping over a dying child, did Paul anguish for the rebellious men in the Corinthian church.

From Clarke's Commentary:
"For out of much affliction, etc. It is very likely that the apostle's enemies had represented him as a harsh, austere, authoritative man; who was better pleased with inflicting wounds than in healing them. But he vindicates himself from this charge by solemnly asserting that this was the most painful part of his office; and that the writing of his first epistle to them cost him much affliction and anguish of heart, and many tears."

5 But if any have caused grief, he hath not grieved me, but in part: that I may not overcharge you all.

... he hath not grieved me, but in part... Paraphrased, this expression is worded thus: "He has grieved me, but he hasn't consumed me with grief. I address him alone. I do not charge any of you other than him." I believe it too easy to simply accept the contention of many that the incestuous person that Paul addressed in I Corinthians is here intended. The Corinthian church was composed entirely of former idol worshippers, so any number of horrendous practices could have been addressed.

Clarke's Commentary has a different opinion on this expression: "Grieved me, but in part - I cannot help thinking that the εκ μερους and απο μερους, which we render in part, and which the apostle uses so frequently in these epistles, are to be referred to the people.

A part of them had acknowledged the apostle, 2Cor 1:14; and here, a part of them had given him cause of grief; and therefore he immediately adds, that I may not overcharge you all; as only a part of you has put me to pain, (viz. the transgressor, and those who had taken his part), it would be unreasonable that I should load you all, επιβαρω παντας ὑμας, with the blame which attaches to that party alone."

6 Sufficient to such a man is this punishment, which was inflicted of many.

Paul advised that the man had been punished enough. Punishment and beating are two words not closely akin. No one can be cured of wrongdoing through beatings. Punishment for wrongdoing may be necessary; over-punishment is never right.

7 So that contrariwise ye ought rather to forgive him, and comfort him, lest perhaps such a one should be swallowed up with overmuch sorrow.

This verse strengthens my opinion that the incestuous fornicator thoroughly dealt with in Paul's first epistle to the Corinthians is not here intended. In I Corinthians 5:3, we read: *For I verily, as absent in body, but present in spirit, have judged already, as though I were present, concerning him that hath so done this deed.* And in verses 4 and 5 of that same chapter, these words appear: *In the name of our Lord Jesus Christ, when ye are gathered together, and my spirit, with the power of our Lord Jesus Christ, 5: To deliver such an one unto Satan for the destruction of the flesh, that the in the day of the Lord Jesus.*

Paul delivered the incestuous fornicator to Satan for the destruction of the flesh. In the interim that separated the 2 epistles, did he then realize his advice to be wrong? He listed 3 authorities in verse four: 1. Lord Jesus Christ; 2. "my" spirit; 3. when ye are gathered together.

Speculation has surrounded the expression "destruction of the flesh." I believe it to mean a physical death, as in the words, *destruction of the flesh.* There is no evidence of a grace period bet-

-ween the judgment of the man and the death of him. In Paul's mind there appeared to be hope that the man would repent at death. His words, *spirit may be saved.* "May be," two words, is definite, while "maybe" leaves doubt. To contend that Paul wrote, may be, to mean that the man would be saved, is erroneous. The words, may be and anything, are always written as 2 words in both Corinthian Epistles.

Does he then in this chapter advise them to forgive such a person? Paul could not have solved every problem that would arise in that heathen-to-Christianity church. We are preserved 2 epistles he wrote to that church, but we are not preserved everything he sent by others.

8 Wherefore I beseech you that ye would confirm your love toward him.
9 For to this end also did I write, that I might know the proof of you, whether ye be obedient in all things.

When Paul penned the words, I did write, surely, he must have referred to another letter he had written to confirm that they had obeyed the instructions in his first epistle. In verse 9, he used the past tense for the verb do as did, signifying another letter had been sent by him. Twice her wrote: "This is the third time I am coming to you" (II Cor. 12:14; 13:1). Many believe that the expressions describe letters.

10 To whom ye forgive any thing, I forgive also: for if I forgave any thing, to whom I forgave it, for your sakes forgave I it in the person of Christ;
11 Lest Satan should get an advantage of us: for we are not ignorant of his devices.

Forgive the incestuous fornicator? I believe that Paul addressed another man in another serious situation—one serious enough to warrant temporary disfellowship but not necessarily excommunication.

12 Furthermore, when I came to Troas to preach Christ's gospel, and a door was opened unto me of the Lord,
13 I had no rest in my spirit, because I found not Titus my brother: but taking my leave of them, I went from thence into

Macedonia.

I came to Troas to preach Christ's gospel, and a door was opened unto me of the Lord, (verse 12). This clause is incomplete without the addition of the words, *I had no rest in my spirit.* Paul went to Troas to preach, and a door was opened for him. But...he was so deeply concerned about the Corinthian church that he could not rest. Titus was to have brought him that news, but his arrival had been delayed. How Paul could have located him in all of Macedonia assaults the imagination. All this demonstrates the immense love he carried for the Corinthians.

The Popular New Testament supplies the following:
"Now when I came to Troas—probably not the city only, but the region of 'the Troad.' It lay on the coast of Mysia, and commercially its importance was considerable,—for the gospel of Christ, and a door was opened unto me of the Lord (compare 1Co 16:9). His object was to take advantage of this journey for missionary purposes, and the field here being open and rich for such work, he would fain have made some stay in it, but for his feverish anxiety for tidings from Corinth, of which he was disappointed by his not finding Titus waiting him there, as he expected."

From Clarke's Commentary on this verse:
"When I came to Troas - After having written the former epistle, and not having heard what effect it had produced on your minds; though the Lord had opened me a particular door to preach the Gospel, in which I so especially rejoice and glory;"

14 Now thanks be unto God, which always causeth us to triumph in Christ, and maketh manifest the savour of his knowledge by us in every place.

I include here 2 lengthy comments from 2 different commentaries that are so rich with information concerning triumphs with the Romans. Paul must have witnessed some of those occasions.

So worthy of a reader's time is Clarke's Commentary's vivid description of verse 14:

"Now, thanks be unto God - His coming dispelled all my fears, and was the cause of the highest satisfaction to my mind; and filled my heart with gratitude to God, who is the Author of all good, and who always causes us to triumph in Christ; not only gives us the victory, but such a victory as involves the total ruin of our enemies; and gives us cause of triumphing in him, through whom we have obtained this victory."

"A triumph, among the Romans, to which the apostle here alludes, was a public and solemn honor conferred by them on a victorious general, by allowing him a magnificent procession through the city."

"This was not granted by the senate unless the general had gained a very signal and decisive victory; conquered a province, etc. On such occasions the general was usually clad in a rich purple robe, interwoven with figures of gold, setting forth the grandeur of his achievements; his buskins were beset with pearls, and he wore a crown, which at first was of laurel, but was afterwards of pure gold. In one hand he had a branch of laurel, the emblem of victory; and in the other, his truncheon. He was carried in a magnificent chariot, adorned with ivory and plates of gold, and usually drawn by two white horses. (Other animals were also used: when Pompey triumphed over Africa, his chariot was drawn by elephants; that of Mark Antony, by lions; that of Heliogabalus, by tigers; and that of Aurelius, by deer.) His children either sat at his feet in the chariot, or rode on the chariot horses. To keep him humble amidst these great honors a slave stood at his back, casting out incessant railings, and reproaches; and carefully enumerating all his vices, etc."

Musicians led up the procession, and played triumphal pieces in praise of the general; and these were followed by young men, who led the victims which were to be sacrificed on the occasion, with their horns gilded, and their heads and necks adorned with ribbons and garlands.

Next followed carts loaded with the spoils taken from the enemy, with their horses, chariots, etc. These were followed by the kings, princes, or generals taken in the war, loaded with chains. Immediately after these came the triumphal chariot, before which, as it passed, the people strewed flowers, and shouted *Io, triumphe*!

"The triumphal chariot was followed by the senate; and the procession was closed by the priests and their attendants, with the different sacrificial utensils, and a white ox, which was to be the chief victim. They then passed through the triumphal arch, along the via sacra to the capitol, where the victims were slain. During this time all the temples were opened, and every altar smoked with offerings and incense."

"The people at Corinth were sufficiently acquainted with the nature of a triumph: about two hundred years before this, Lucius Mummius, the Roman consul, had conquered all Achaia, destroyed Corinth, Thebes, and Chalcis; and, by order of the senate, had a grand triumph, and was surnamed Achaicus. St. Paul had now a triumph (but of a widely different kind) over the same people; his triumph was in Christ, and to Christ he gives all the glory; his sacrifice was that of thanksgiving to his Lord; and the incense offered on the occasion caused the savour of the knowledge of Christ to be manifested in every place."

"As the smoke of the victims and incense offered on such an occasion would fill the whole city with their perfume, so the odor of the name and doctrine of Christ filled the whole of Corinth and the neighboring regions; and the apostles appeared as triumphing in and through Christ, over devils, idols, superstition, ignorance, and vice, wherever they came."

Jamieson-Fausset-Brown Commentary:
"causeth us to triumph — The *Greek,* is rather, as in Col 2:15, "triumphs over us": "leadeth us in triumph." Paul regarded himself as a signal trophy of God's victorious power in Christ. His Almighty Conqueror was leading him about, through all the cities of the Greek and Roman world, as an illustrious example of His power at once to subdue and to save. The foe of Christ was now the servant of Christ. As to be led in triumph by man is the most miserable, so to be led in triumph by God is the most glorious, lot that can befall any [Trench].

Our only true triumphs are God's triumphs over us. His defeats of us are our only true victories [Alford]. The image is taken from the triumphal procession of a victorious general. The *additional* idea is perhaps included, which distinguishes God's triumph from that of a human general, that the captive is brought into *willing obedience* (2Co 10:5) to Christ, and so *joins in the triumph:* God 'leads him in triumph' as one not merely *triumphed over,* but also as one *triumphing over* God's foes with God (which last will apply to the apostle's triumphant missionary progress under the leading of God). So Bengel: "*Who shows us in triumph,* not [merely] as conquered, but as the ministers of His victory. Not only the victory, but the open 'showing' of the victory is marked: for there follows, *Who maketh manifest.*'

"savour — retaining the image of a triumph. As the approach of the triumphal procession was made known by the *odor* of incense scattered far and wide by the incense-bearers in the train, so God 'makes manifest by us' (His now at once triumphed over and triumphing captives, compare Luke 5:10, "'Catch,' literally, 'Take captive so as to preserve alive') the sweet savor of the knowledge of Christ, the triumphant Conqueror (Col 2:15), everywhere. As the *triumph* strikes the eyes, so the savor the nostrils; thus every sense feels the power of Christ's Gospel. This *manifestation* (a word often recurring in his Epistles to the Corinthians, compare 1Co 4:5) refutes the Corinthian suspicions of his *dishonestly,* by reserve, *hiding* anything from them (2Co 2:17; 2Co 4:2)."

15 For we are unto God a sweet savour of Christ, in them that are saved, and in them that perish:
16 To the one we are the savour of death unto death; and to the other the savour of life unto life. And who is sufficient for these things?

The noun "savor" denotes the taste or smell of something—a particular smell or taste, or the distinctive quality or taste of something.

The verb "savor" may be described as "to taste or to smell something".

Translators did well in choosing savour (British spelling of savor). Christians may exude a pleasant or noxious savor. However, a noxious taste or smell always offends and always produces rejection.

"We are the savour of death unto death - We are the occasion of deepening their condemnation, and of sinking them lower into ruin. The expression used here means literally, 'to the one class we bear a death-conveying odor leading to their death' - a savor, a smell which, under the circumstances, is destructive to life, and which leads to death. Mr. Locke renders this: 'To the one my preaching is of ill savor, unacceptable and offensive, by their rejecting whereof they draw death on themselves.' Grateful as their labors were to God, and acceptable as would be their efforts, whatever might be the results, yet Paul could not be ignorant that the gospel would in fact be the means of greater condemnation to many. It was indeed by their own fault; yet wherever the gospel was preached, it would to many have this result. It is probable that the language here used is borrowed from similar expressions which were common among the Jews." (Barnes)

17 For we are not as many, which corrupt the word of God: but as of sincerity, but as of God, in the sight of God speak we in Christ.

Paul intended here to convey that the false teachers in Corinth were far more numerous than the Apostle and his followers were. Paul and his followers delivered truth, while false teachers expounded a corrupt (rotten, spoiled) doctrine. This definition is applicable to both heathen doctrines and, also, to the corrupted message that "false brethren crept in unaware" spread abroad.

...but as of sincerity, but as of God, in the sight of God speak we in Christ.

Of sincerity—of God—in Christ: These words describe Paul's entire ministry. And so must they describe every ministry in order for them to be sanctioned and certified by God.

Bob Koonce Th. D.

CHAPTER THREE

1 Do we begin again to commend ourselves? or need we, as some others, epistles of commendation to you, or letters of commendation from you?

2 Ye are our epistle written in our hearts, known and read of all men:

3 Forasmuch as ye are manifestly declared to be the epistle of Christ ministered by us, written not with ink, but with the Spirit of the living God; not in tables of stone, but in fleshy tables of the heart.

4 And such trust have we through Christ to God-ward:

5 Not that we are sufficient of ourselves to think any thing as of ourselves; but our sufficiency is of God;

6 ¶ Who also hath made us able ministers of the new testament; not of the letter, but of the spirit: for the letter killeth, but the spirit giveth life.

7 But if the ministration of death, written and engraven in stones, was glorious, so that the children of Israel could not stedfastly behold the face of Moses for the glory of his countenance; which glory was to be done away:

8 How shall not the ministration of the spirit be rather glorious?

9 For if the ministration of condemnation be glory, much more doth the ministration of righteousness exceed in glory.

10 For even that which was made glorious had no glory in this respect, by reason of the glory that excelleth.

11 For if that which is done away was glorious, much more that which remaineth is glorious.

12 Seeing then that we have such hope, we use great plainness of speech:

13 And not as Moses, which put a vail over his face, that the children of Israel could not stedfastly look to the end of that which is abolished:

14 But their minds were blinded: for until this day remaineth the same vail untaken away in the reading of the old testament; which vail is done away in Christ.

15 But even unto this day, when Moses is read, the vail is upon their heart.
16 Nevertheless when it shall turn to the Lord, the vail shall be taken away.
17 Now the Lord is that Spirit: and where the Spirit of the Lord is, there is liberty.
18 But we all, with open face beholding as in a glass the glory of the Lord, are changed into the same image from glory to glory, even as by the Spirit of the Lord.

The essence of this chapter is an effort to change the mindset of the Corinthian church from carnality to spirituality. Though greater in number than the dissenters, the faithful persons still seemed somewhat reticent about totally accepting Paul's authority as being ordained by God.

1 Do we begin again to commend ourselves? or need we, as some others, epistles of commendation to you, or letters of commendation from you?
2 Ye are our epistle written in our hearts, known and read of all men:
3 Forasmuch as ye are manifestly declared to be the epistle of Christ ministered by us, written not with ink, but with the Spirit of the living God; not in tables of stone, but in fleshy tables of the heart.

So early, as in this instance, letters of recommendation appear to already have been in use. *Do we begin again to commend ourselves?* Paul's words here say, "Do we have to start all over again? Do we have to brag on ourselves? ... *need we, as some others, epistles* (letters) recommending us? You are our letter of recommendation. You are living witnesses to the effect of our ministry.

4 And such trust have we through Christ to God-ward:

"And such trust have we - Such confidence have we that we are appointed by God, and that He accepts our work. Such evidence have we in the success of our labors; such irrefragable proof that God blesses us; that we have trust, or confidence, that we are sent by God, and are owned by him in our ministry. His confidence did not rest on letters of introduction from people, but in the evidence of the divine presence, and the divine acceptance of his work." (Barnes)

5 Not that we are sufficient of ourselves to think any thing as of ourselves; but our sufficiency is of God;

Paul was careful not to credit himself. He endeavored always to give all glory and praise to God. He wrote that the Corinthian Christians were his epistle, but Jesus Christ was the real author of their epistle. That epistle was not written with ink, but with the Spirit of the living God. It was not written on tablets of stone. God's promise for New Testament Christians is contained in the words, *I will take away the stony heart, and I will give you a heart of flesh*, (a human heart-Ezekiel 36:26).

6 ¶ Who also hath made us able ministers of the new testament; not of the letter, but of the spirit: for the letter killeth, but the spirit giveth life.

Ministers: Servers; servants; never lords. The Law of Moses designated Priests and Levites *to serve* the people. Through the Priests, the letter of the Law was given to the people. God used Paul and other apostles and prophets to preach the *Spirit* of the New Testament.

7 But if the ministration of death, written and engraven in stones, was glorious, so that the children of Israel could not stedfastly behold the face of Moses for the glory of his countenance; which glory was to be done away:
8 How shall not the ministration of the spirit be rather glorious?

In verse 7, Paul made a comparison between the Old Testament and the New, the Law of Moses and the Gospel of Jesus Christ. He viewed this as endorsing the claim by him, that he and his fellow-labourers were able ministers of the New Testament.

...ministration of death, written and engraven in stones... Legality, as in the words, *the letter killeth, but the Spirit giveth life.* The design of the Law was to produce condemnation. In Romans 7:9, Paul wrote, *...but when the commandment came, sin revived,*

and I died.

But if the ministration of death, written and engraven in stones, was glorious...describes the glory of God's presence on Mt. Sinai where Moses was given the Law. Though Mt. Sinai was clothed in darkness, Moses' face glowed when he came down from the mount. The people of Israel could not view his face because of its brightness. So great was the glory on his face that Moses was forced to veil his face before the people of Israel could look at him. And as God chose to show His glory on Moses' face, so did He choose to veil it with flesh in the person of Jesus Christ.

How shall not the ministration of the spirit be rather glorious? The word, rather, used here should have been, more. The ministration of the Spirit is <u>more</u> glorious. This is confirmed in the next verse.

9 For if the ministration of condemnation be glory, much more doth the ministration of righteousness exceed in glory.

Paul here continued his assault on false teachers in the church who persuaded others to abide by the Law. "If then," he could have written, "the Law that offered nothing but condemnation seems to thrill you, you must realize that grace by Jesus Christ does so much more thrill a child of God."

10 For even that which was made glorious had no glory in this respect, by reason of the glory that excelleth.

Simply said, the Law of Moses had no glory in itself. It could never have been credited with glory in any scale had it not been for the death, burial, and resurrection of Jesus Christ. The Law was instituted for one specific purpose—to bring condemnation on all mankind—on everyone before the Law was instituted and on everyone afterward. For that reason, we read: *For God so loved the world, that he gave his only begotten Son, that whosoever believeth in him should not perish, but have everlasting life* (John 3:16).

11 For if that which is done away was glorious, much more that which remaineth is glorious.

12 Seeing then that we have such hope, we use great plainness of speech:

...that which is done away was glorious... Paul used the past tense of the verb, is. The Law was. It had been, but it no longer <u>was</u>. It became fulfilled in Jesus Christ. God didn't destroy the Law; He replaced it. *For by grace are ye saved through faith; and that not of yourselves: it is the gift of God:* (Ephesians 2:8)

...we use great plainness of speech: Paul was well educated. He could have employed words and language that lesser-learned people could not have understood. Rather, he used plain, everyday language. The message of hope in Jesus Christ is far too important to be lost in a jumble of words.

Clarke's Commentary gives a very pertinent explanation of this phrase:
"We speak not only with all confidence, but with all imaginable plainness; keeping back nothing; disguising nothing; concealing nothing: and here we differ greatly from the Jewish doctors, and from the Gentile philosophers, who affect obscurity, and endeavor, by figures, metaphors, and allegories, to hide everything from the vulgar. But we wish that all may hear; and we speak so that all may understand." My note: The word, vulgar, originally meant "common" and people of low estate were referred to as vulgar (common)."

13 And not as Moses, which put a vail over his face, that the children of Israel could not stedfastly look to the end of that which is abolished:

This verse continues the thought "great plainness of speech" in verse 12. The message Paul preached, he asserted, was not veiled, not obscured, not hidden. The children of Israel could not *steadfastly*--could not maintain a prolonged gaze at Moses because his face shone too brightly. His message, he asserted, did not blind, bind, or enslave his listeners.

14 But their minds were blinded: for until this day remaineth the same vail untaken away in the reading of the old testament; which

vail is done away in Christ.
15 But even unto this day, when Moses is read, the vail is upon their heart.

As Moses' face was veiled to hide the glory upon it, so does a veil still remain on the minds and hearts of adherents of Judaism. According to Paul's words, the veil still obscures the reading of the Old Testament.

16 Nevertheless when it shall turn to the Lord, the vail shall be taken away.

The word, it, in this verse can be understood to mean, "when it- the mind and heart, shall turn to the Lord." It could also be interpreted as, "when it, the Jewish people, shall turn to the Lord." The latter application is the most correct.

Barnes Notes on the New Testament give this on verse 16:
Nevertheless - This is not always to continue. The time is coming when they shall understand their own Scriptures, and see their true beauty.

When it shall turn to the Lord - When the Jewish people shall be converted. The word "it" here refers undoubtedly to "Israel."

17 Now the Lord is that Spirit: and where the Spirit of the Lord is, there is liberty.

I was somewhat intrigued as I scanned comments on this verse in several commentaries. The question as to which Spirit was intended in this verse was presented. If a person believes there to be more than one Spirit in the Godhead, then he or she does indeed need to search for the identity of the Spirit in verse 17:

John 4:24 gives us: *God is a Spirit: and they that worship him must worship him in spirit and in truth.*

Verse 17 gives us: *Now the Lord is that Spirit:*

One Lord, one faith, one baptism (Ephesians 4:5)

And they say unto her, Woman, why weepest thou? She saith unto them, Because they have taken away my Lord, and I know not where they have laid him (John 20:13).

Therefore that disciple whom Jesus loved saith unto Peter, It is the Lord. Now when Simon Peter heard that it was the Lord, he girt his fisher's coat unto him, (for he was naked,) and did cast himself into the sea (John 21:7).

Jesus saith unto them, Come and dine. And none of the disciples durst ask him, Who art thou? knowing that it was the Lord (John 21:12).

18 But we all, with open face beholding as in a glass the glory of the Lord, are changed into the same image from glory to glory, even as by the Spirit of the Lord.

In my mind, the words, *which vail is done away in Christ* (verse 14), bear heavily on this verse. At first glance, verse 18 seems orphaned from previous verses. However, when the veil is taken away by Jesus Christ, we view Him so differently. At first glance at a mirror, many of our blemishes are unapparent, but as we continue to gaze, we discover blemishes we wish weren't there. And that, the true message of this verse seems apparent.

As we look more and more at our earthly possessions, the less enticing they become to us. But as we look more intently at Jesus, the more valuable He becomes to us!

Bob Koonce Th. D.

CHAPTER FOUR

1 Therefore seeing we have this ministry, as we have received mercy, we faint not;

2 But have renounced the hidden things of dishonesty, not walking in craftiness, nor handling the word of God deceitfully; but by manifestation of the truth commending ourselves to every man's conscience in the sight of God.

3 But if our gospel be hid, it is hid to them that are lost:

4 In whom the god of this world hath blinded the minds of them which believe not, lest the light of the glorious gospel of Christ, who is the image of God, should shine unto them.

5 For we preach not ourselves, but Christ Jesus the Lord; and ourselves your servants for Jesus' sake.

6 For God, who commanded the light to shine out of darkness, hath shined in our hearts, to give the light of the knowledge of the glory of God in the face of Jesus Christ.

7 But we have this treasure in earthen vessels, that the excellency of the power may be of God, and not of us.

8 We are troubled on every side, yet not distressed; we are perplexed, but not in despair;

9 Persecuted, but not forsaken; cast down, but not destroyed;

10 Always bearing about in the body the dying of the Lord Jesus, that the life also of Jesus might be made manifest in our body.

11 For we which live are alway delivered unto death for Jesus' sake, that the life also of Jesus might be made manifest in our mortal flesh.

12 So then death worketh in us, but life in you.

13 We having the same spirit of faith, according as it is written, I believed, and therefore have I spoken; we also believe, and therefore speak;

14 Knowing that he which raised up the Lord Jesus shall raise up us also by Jesus, and shall present us with you.

15 For all things are for your sakes, that the abundant grace might through the thanksgiving of many redound to the glory of God.

16 For which cause we faint not; but though our outward man perish, yet the inward man is renewed day by day.
17 For our light affliction, which is but for a moment, worketh for us a far more exceeding and eternal weight of glory;
18 While we look not at the things which are seen, but at the things which are not seen: for the things which are seen are temporal; but the things which are not seen are eternal.

Verse 18, the last verse of the previous chapter 3, introduces this chapter: *But we all, with open face beholding as in a glass the glory of the Lord, are changed into the same image from glory to glory, even as by the Spirit of the Lord.*

When the image we see in life's mirror ceases to reflect us and, instead, reflects Jesus, we will have taken on the nature of Christ. Truth turns carnal attractions into trash. The brilliance of the glory that surrounds our Lord Jesus blinds a Christian's eyes to see nothing other than the Lord. To be a Christian is to be changed. It is that thought that introduces "therefore" the first word in verse 1 of this chapter.

1 Therefore seeing we have this ministry, as we have received mercy, we faint not;

Therefore... because of; due to the fact; for this reason. Before his conversion, Paul had pursued a far different course for his life. He breathed extreme hatred for Christians and persecuted them cruelly. It was the Jesus he vehemently despised that stopped and transformed him on his journey to persecute the Christians in Damascus, Syria. Having seen the Lord and been given instructions by the Lord, his one message was a crucified Jesus Christ and a resurrected Jesus Christ. His message never changed. He wrote, "For me to live is Christ, and to die is gain."

"Therefore - Διὰ τοῦτο Dia touto. On account of this. That is, because the light of the gospel is so clear; because it reveals so glorious truths, and all obscurity is taken away, and we are permitted to behold as in a mirror the glory of the Lord, 2Cor. 3:18. Since the glories of the gospel dispensation are so great, and its effects on the heart are so transforming and purifying. The ob-

-ject is, to show the "effect" of being entrusted with such a ministry, on the character of his preaching." (Barnes)

...as we have received mercy... This phrase, standing alone, would yield the connotation, "as we have received, so we give." That is a wrong interpretation. The sense of the phrase is, "since; because; due to the fact." The verse, thus written, would then read: *Due to the fact we have* (or because we) *have received mercy, we faint not; Therefore, we have this ministry.*

2 But have renounced the hidden things of dishonesty, not walking in craftiness, nor handling the word of God deceitfully; but by manifestation of the truth commending ourselves to every man's conscience in the sight of God.

But have renounced the hidden things of dishonesty... I insert the phrase *"we have received mercy"* from verse 1 into this phrase. By this addition, a complete sentence would read; *But we have received mercy* and *have renounced the hidden things of dishonesty*:

The Merriam-Webster Collegiate Dictionary gives the following definitions for "renounce":
"To refuse to follow, obey, or recognize in any way." When applied to an ecclesiastical body, renounce means to separate from, to refute any further authority of that religious organization.

Paul listed three things he and his helpers had renounced:
- *the hidden things of dishonesty:* Sneakiness is dishonest.
- *not walking in craftiness:* Deceitful actions in a crafty, hidden manner.
- *nor handling the word of God deceitfully:* Hypocritical
-

"But have renounced - Απειπαμεθα· We have disclaimed the hidden things of dishonesty; τα κρυπτα της αισχυνης, the hidden things of shame; those things which wicked men do; and which they are ashamed to have known, and ashamed to own. Dr. Whitby thinks that the apostle refers to carnal abominations, of which the Jews and their rabbins were notoriously guilty. And it does appear from the first epistle that there were persons in Corinth who taught that fornication was no sin; and it appears also that several had taken the part of the incestuous person." (Clarke)

3 But if our gospel be hid, it is hid to them that are lost:

This verse was directed to those in the Corinthian church who refused Paul's message and authority. He listed their sins in the previous verse 3. The truth that we must gather from this verse is the message that men are lost by choice. The men in that congregation chose to refuse and to refute Paul's message. His words, *if our gospel be hid,* imply a determination of some in that church to reject the message of salvation that Paul preached, simply because it was Paul that preached it.

Clarke's Commentary offers the following:
"But if our Gospel be hid - Κεκαλυμμενον· Veiled; he refers to the subject that he had treated so particularly in the conclusion of the preceding chapter. If there be a veil on the Gospel, it is only to the willfully blind…"

Paul continued to expose the error and the condition of the willfully blind to the Gospel in the next verse:

4 In whom the god of this world hath blinded the minds of them which believe not, lest the light of the glorious gospel of Christ, who is the image of God, should shine unto them.

No person is his/her own master. Every sinner is already a bonded servant of the devil. Jesus said: *"No man can serve two masters: for either he will hate the one, and love the other; or else he will hold to the one, and despise the other. Ye cannot serve God and mammon* (Matthew 6:24).

In whom the god of this world-Satan, called a "god" in this verse, is not a real god at all. He is a pretender, a wannabe God. The word, god, is not capitalized in this verse. Satan is not a real god, merely an impostor of God. Still, he possesses great power, so much so that Michael, the archangel, imposed the Power of God upon him (Jude, verse 9): *Yet Michael the archangel, when contending with the devil he disputed about the body of Moses, durst not bring against him a railing accusation, but said, The Lord rebuke thee.*

Christ, who is the <u>image</u> of God... (verse 4)
Who being the brightness of his glory, and the express image of his person, and upholding all things by the word of his power, when he had by himself purged our sins, sat down on the right hand of the Majesty on high (Hebrews 1:3);
Colossians 1:15 Who is the image of the invisible God, the firstborn of every creature
Hebrews 1:3 *Who being the brightness of his glory, and the express image of his person, and upholding all things by the word of his power, when he had by himself purged our sins, sat down on the right hand of the Majesty on high;*

5 For we preach not ourselves, but Christ Jesus the Lord; and ourselves your servants for Jesus' sake.

From Adam Clarke:
"For we preach not ourselves but Christ Jesus the Lord - We proclaim the author of this glorious Gospel as Christ, ὁ Χριστος, the same as המשיח hammashiach, the Messiah, the Anointed One; him of whom the prophets wrote; and who is the expectation, as he is the glory, of Israel, We proclaim him as Jesus, Savior and Deliverer, who saves men from their sins. See Matt.1:21. And we proclaim Jesus of Nazareth to be the long-expected Messiah; and that there will be none other. And farther we proclaim this Jesus the Messiah to be the Lord, ὁ Κυριος, the great Ruler who has all power in heaven and earth; who made and governs the world; and who can save to the uttermost all that come to God through him. Such was the Redeemer preached by St. Paul." AMEN!

...and ourselves your servants for Jesus' sake. In my opinion, this expression is awkwardly worded. The Apostle, and those with him, would not have preached themselves. "Being servants of Christ, they preached Jesus Christ" is the intended meaning of the phrase.

6 For God, who commanded the light to shine out of darkness, hath shined in our hearts, to give the light of the knowledge of the glory of God in the face of Jesus Christ.

For God, who commanded <u>the</u> <u>light</u> to shine out of darkness... Paul refers here to Genesis 1:3: *And God said, Let there be light: and there was light.* John, chapter 1, verses 1-5, reads:

1 In the beginning was the Word, and the Word was with God, and the Word was God.
2 The same was in the beginning with God.
3 All things were made by him; and without him was not anything made that was made.
4 In him was life; and the <u>life</u> was the <u>light</u> of men.
5 And the light shineth in darkness; and the darkness comprehended it not.

The word, light, in verse 5 refers to Jesus Christ. "The darkness comprehended it not" links with John 1:11: *He came unto his own, and his own received him not.*

Rev. 3:14: And unto the angel of the church of the Laodiceans write; These things saith the Amen, the faithful and true witness, the beginning of the creation of God;

For God, who commanded the light to shine out of darkness, hath shined in our hearts, to give the light of the knowledge of the glory of God in the face of Jesus Christ (verse 6 once more). If must be understood that God is Light, and in Him is no darkness at all! It is God Who pierced darkness in the beginning, and Who brought Light to "whosoever will" in the person of Jesus Christ. When people surrender their blackened hearts to Jesus Christ, the Light of the glory of God dispels every shred of darkness from their souls.

7 But we have this treasure in earthen vessels, that the excellency of the power may be of God, and not of us.

According to Clarke's Commentary, the original Greek term, οστρακινοις σκευεσιν, signifies, more literally, vessels made of shells, which are very brittle. I believe this to be an excellent application comparable to our bodies. "From dust thou art, and to dust shall thou return." And like brittle shells, humans do break. That God would allow a human being to possess such a treasured gift as the Holy Ghost- the Spirit of a resurrected Christ, defies human reasoning.

...that the excellency of the power may be of God, and not of us. The power of God is here described as excellent. It is perfect, without fault, indestructible. This phrase so perfectly describes the love and mercy of God. Unlike God, humans are imperfect, are full of faults, and certainly are destructible. Paul so beautifully attributes all the glory to the wondrous God Who entrusts such an invaluable gift as the Holy Ghost to mortal man.

8 We are troubled on every side, yet not distressed; we are perplexed, but not in despair;
9 Persecuted, but not forsaken; cast down, but not destroyed;

The Word of God is so beautiful, so perfect, so indisputable, so powerful, and so ever on time every time. Verses 8 and 9 beckon and embrace a promise of God, found in First Corinthians 10:13: *There hath no temptation taken you but such as is common to man: but God is faithful, who will not suffer you to be tempted above that ye are able; but will with the temptation also make a way to escape, that ye may be able to bear it.* It was Paul who penned this verse, generated apparently from personal experience.

We are troubled on every side, yet not distressed;
We are *perplexed, but not in despair;*
We are *persecuted, but not forsaken;*
We are *cast down, but not destroyed* - May God forgive us who live comfortably, forgive us when we complain!

"We are troubled on every side,.... Or afflicted; εν παντι, either 'in every place', wherever we are, into whatsoever country, city, or town we enter, we are sure to meet with trouble, of one sort or another; for wherever we be, we are in the world, in which we must expect tribulation: or 'always', every day and hour we live, as in 2Cor.4:10 we are never free from one trial or another: or 'by everyone'; by all sorts of persons, good and bad, professors and profane, open persecutors and false brethren; yea, some of the dear children of God, weak believers, give us trouble: or 'with every sort' of trouble, inward and outward; trouble from the world, the flesh and the devil:" (Gill)

10 Always bearing about in the body the dying of the Lord Jesus, that the life also of Jesus might be made manifest in our body.

Always bearing about in the body... With his body scarred from the cruel beating that he suffered at Philippi and an earlier stoning that left him for dead, Paul could identify with the beating and death of the Lord Jesus. The verse doesn't end there, however. He added, *that the life also of Jesus might be made manifest in our body.* "Why would a man jeopardize his own life preaching about a dead man?" must have been asked. That question afforded Paul the opportunity to preach a resurrected, living Christ who will ultimately judge the world.

11 For we which live are alway delivered unto death for Jesus' sake, that the life also of Jesus might be made manifest in our mortal flesh.

"Always and in all places and circumstances are we subject to arrest, torture, and death. We are willing to die for Jesus Christ."

12 So then death worketh in us, but life in you.

"We exist with our lives constantly threatened, but such has been the case since, and even before we brought the message of eternal lie to you and to others.

13 We having the same spirit of faith, according as it is written, I believed, and therefore have I spoken; we also believe, and therefore speak;

Jeremiah wrote in chapter 20, verse 9 of his book these words:
Then I said, I will not make mention of him, nor speak any more in his name. But his word was in mine heart as a burning fire shut up in my bones, and I was weary with forbearing, and I could not stay. Paul said, "we also believe, and therefore speak."

14 Knowing that he which raised up the Lord Jesus shall raise up us also by Jesus, and shall present us with you.

Knowing... "There's no doubt...He Who raised Jesus from death...shall raise us (Paul and his companions) by Jesus...and we will appear together.

15 For all things are for your sakes, that the abundant grace might through the thanksgiving of many redound to the glory of God.

"Everything we do and preach is for your benefit so that grace in abundance is generated by the thanksgiving of many saints to the glory of God."

16 For which cause we faint not; but though our outward man perish, yet the inward man is renewed day by day.

For which cause we faint not... "We don't give up. Our bodies weary, but our spirits are strengthened daily, day by day.".

17 For our light affliction, which is but for a moment, worketh for us a far more exceeding and eternal weight of glory;

...our light affliction, After the whippings, beatings, stoning, and hunger that he and others with him had already suffered, it is amazing that Paul would describe it all as light affliction. This will once again face the Church. Can we then term our sufferings as "light afflictions"?

18 While we look not at the things which are seen, but at the things which are not seen: for the things which are seen are temporal; but the things which are not seen are eternal.

In this verse, Paul explains his usage of the term "light" in describing affliction. He said, "We don't look at things we see that will pass away—we look for eternal things that we cannot now see."

Bob Koonce Th. D.

CHAPTER FIVE

1For we know that if our earthly house of this tabernacle were dissolved, we have a building of God, an house not made with hands, eternal in the heavens.

2 For in this we groan, earnestly desiring to be clothed upon with our house which is from heaven:

3 If so be that being clothed we shall not be found naked.

4 For we that are in this tabernacle do groan, being burdened: not for that we would be unclothed, but clothed upon, that mortality might be swallowed up of life.

5 Now he that hath wrought us for the selfsame thing is God, who also hath given unto us the earnest of the Spirit.

6 Therefore we are always confident, knowing that, whilst we are at home in the body, we are absent from the Lord:

7 (For we walk by faith, not by sight:)

8 We are confident, I say, and willing rather to be absent from the body, and to be present with the Lord.

9 Wherefore we labour, that, whether present or absent, we may be accepted of him.

10 For we must all appear before the judgment seat of Christ; that every one may receive the things done in his body, according to that he hath done, whether it be good or bad.

11 Knowing therefore the terror of the Lord, we persuade men; but we are made manifest unto God; and I trust also are made manifest in your consciences.

12 For we commend not ourselves again unto you, but give you occasion to glory on our behalf, that ye may have somewhat to answer them which glory in appearance, and not in heart.

13 For whether we be beside ourselves, it is to God: or whether we be sober, it is for your cause.

14 For the love of Christ constraineth us; because we thus judge, that if one died for all, then were all dead:

15 And that he died for all, that they which live should not henceforth live unto themselves, but unto him which died for them, and rose again.

16 Wherefore henceforth know we no man after the flesh: yea, though we have known Christ after the flesh, yet now henceforth know we him no more.

17 Therefore if any man be in Christ, he is a new creature: old things are passed away; behold, all things are become new.

18 And all things are of God, who hath reconciled us to himself by Jesus Christ, and hath given to us the ministry of reconciliation;

19 To wit, that God was in Christ, reconciling the world unto himself, not imputing their trespasses unto them; and hath committed unto us the word of reconciliation.

20 Now then we are ambassadors for Christ, as though God did beseech you by us: we pray you in Christ's stead, be ye reconciled to God.

21 For he hath made him to be sin for us, who knew no sin; that we might be made the righteousness of God in him.

In this chapter, Paul pursued the argument of the previous chapter concerning the hope of eternal life with Jesus, which hope explained their courage and patience under afflictions. *Looking for that blessed hope, and the glorious appearing of the great God and our Saviour Jesus Christ*; (Titus 2:13)

1For we know that if our earthly house of this tabernacle were dissolved, we have a building of God, an house not made with hands, eternal in the heavens.

...*our earthly house of this tabernacle*... "house" is to be understood as "body". "tabernacle" is "dwelling place". Thus, the verse conveys the thought that when mortality shall cease and the earth and all the elements shall be done away, God has prepared a tabernacle (place) for our heavenly house (heavenly body) to dwell in. Paul described Heaven in the words: *a building of God, an house not made with hands, eternal in the heavens.* He prefixed that promise with the words: *For we know.* Yes, that promise is a definite!

F.B. Meyer left the following very descriptive words about verse 1: "This mortal life is a pilgrimage, and our body is a tent, so slight, so transitory, so easily taken down; but what does it matter, since there is awaiting us a mansion prepared by God? Often in this veil of flesh we groan. It cages us, anchors us down to earth, hampers us with its needs, obstructs our vision, and becomes the medium of temptation. How good it would be if our physical body could be suddenly transmuted into the glorified ethereal body which should be like the resurrection body of our Lord! It would be sweet to escape the wrench of death. But if not, then through death we shall carry with us the germ of the glorified body. That which shall be quickened will first die, but God will give it a body as it shall please Him.

"The gate of death may look gloomy on this side, but on the other it is of burnished gold, and opens directly into the presence-chamber of Jesus. We long to see Him and to be with Him; and such desires are the work of the Holy Spirit and the first fruits of heaven. But remember that just inside the door there is Christ's judgment seat, where He will adjudge our life and apportion our reward. Prepare, my soul, to give an account of thy talents!" (F.B. Meyer)

2 For in this we groan, earnestly desiring to be clothed upon with our house which is from heaven:

Paul intended the word, *groan*, to be understood literally. He followed *"groan"* with the word, *earnestly* (intently, *seriously*). As he stated in chapter 4 that he and his helpers grew very weary, were always in danger of torture and death, but they never quit. Still, they *longed* to be delivered from their human bodies, clothed with immortal bodies, and forever be with Jesus.

3 If so be that being clothed we shall not be found naked.

I find 2 verses in Matthew, chapter 22, to be pertinent to this verse:
11 And when the king came in to see the guests, he saw there a man which had not on a wedding garment:
12 And he saith unto him, Friend, how camest thou in hither not having a wedding garment? And he was speechless.

Clarke's Commentary explains verse 3 thus:
If so be that being clothed - That is, fully prepared in this life for

the glory of God;

We shall not be found naked - Destitute in that future state of that Divine image which shall render us capable of enjoying an endless glory.

4 For we that are in this tabernacle do groan, being burdened: not for that we would be unclothed, but clothed upon, that mortality might be swallowed up of life.

This verse is given in addition to the information in verse 2. Again, the Apostle used the word, *groan*. I think there is no evidence that Paul felt dejected, but that he so felt the need to preach to so many that he humanly could not yet reach, that he *groaned* in his spirit.

...being burdened: not for that we would be unclothed, but clothed upon... This was not a death wish; more properly, it speaks of homesickness. *For I am in a strait betwixt two, having a desire to depart, and to be with Christ; which is far better: Nevertheless, to abide in the flesh is more needful for you* (Philippians 1:23, 24).

Nearly every waking moment of Paul's life was filled with concern. There was always the drive to preach, concern for his safety, where, when, how, of if he would next eat. He had no steady income. It appears that he suffered some affliction, for which, three times, he asked healing. God answered that request with the words, "My grace is sufficient for thee."

5 Now he that hath wrought us for the selfsame thing is God, who also hath given unto us the earnest of the Spirit.

...selfsame thing- "the same thing". This expression gets its sense in part from verse 4. God made Adam a perfect being. Sin destroyed that state, but God never intended that sin should become the final victor. It is for that reason we read 2 Peter 3:9: *The Lord is not slack concerning his promise, as some men count slackness; but is longsuffering to us-ward, not willing that any should perish, but that all should come to repentance.* Paul and his companions were wrought (made/ordained) preachers of deliverance from a spiritual death unto an eternal life.

...earnest of the Spirit... The word, earnest, comes from Greek, *aarhabon*. It signifies a pledge, something given as security for the purchase price; part of the purchase price. This verse uses the word, earnest, as *earnest of the Spirit.* Several commentaries, in my opinion, leave incomplete explanations for this phrase. The Matthew Henry Commentary states "earnest of the Spirit" could be rendered as "the believer's earnest desire". Had I lived more than 200 years ago, I might have written something similar. I think the definition for earnest in the first sentence of this paragraph to be accurate.

6 Therefore we are always confident, knowing that, whilst we are at home in the body, we are absent from the Lord:
7 (For we walk by faith, not by sight:)
8 we are always confident, I say, and willing rather to be absent from the body, and to be present with the Lord.

Completely restructured, verses 6 and 7, could be written as: *Being absent from the Lord while at home in the body, we are always confident—for we walk by faith and not by sight.* In verse 8 he repeated the expression; *we are always confident.*

...willing rather to be absent from the body- Homesick for heaven. Rather to be with Jesus than to be further troubled with danger, weariness, hunger, and all the uncertainties of life, Paul longed to go home to and to be with Jesus forever.

9 Wherefore we labour, that, whether present or absent, we may be accepted of him.

To be more properly understood, a rearrangement of this verse would read: *We labor that we may be accepted of him whether present or absent*--that is, whether *dead* or *alive.* Paul intended the verse to covey the truth that it is important to be accepted, pleasing to God all the time. He gave the reason for such a message in the following verse 10.

10 For we must all appear before the judgment seat of Christ; that every one may receive the things done in his body, according to that he hath done, whether it be good or bad.

John 5:28,29 and Revelation 20:11,12 concur with verse 10:

²⁸Marvel not at this: for the hour is coming, in the which all that are in the graves shall hear his voice, ²⁹ And shall come forth; they that have done good, unto the resurrection of life; and they that have done evil, unto the resurrection of damnation.

Revelation 20:11,12: And I saw a great white throne, and him that sat on it, from whose face the earth and the heaven fled away; and there was found no place for them.
¹²And I saw the dead, small and great, stand before God; and the books were opened: and another book was opened, which is the book of life: and the dead were judged out of those things which were written in the books, according to their works.

11 Knowing therefore the terror of the Lord, we persuade men; but we are made manifest unto God; and I trust also are made manifest in your consciences.

...terror of the Lord. I believe that the usage of terror relating to fear of the final Judgment of all mankind is the correct word. Adam Clarke's Commentary disagrees: "This, I think," he wrote, "is too harsh a translation of ειδοτες ουν τον φοβον του Κυριου, which should be rendered, knowing therefore the fear of the Lord;"

Merriam-Webster Collegiate Dictionary describes "terror" as: a state of intense fear. James 2:19 gives the words: *Thou believest that there is one God; thou doest well: the devils also believe, and tremble.* The comparison is here made of our belief of God and the devils' belief of the same God. Devils tremble because they are forever lost; should not unsaved people not merely fear, but fear to the point that they tremble, knowing they will share the same fate that faces devils?

12 For we commend not ourselves again unto you, but give you occasion to glory on our behalf, that ye may have somewhat to answer them which glory in appearance, and not in heart.

For we commend not ourselves again. I think that Paul here speaks of information of success he and his companions had recently experienced. The information was included not to persuade them to better respect and accept him. It was intended to give them evidence of the success of Paul, their pastor, and proof that the Gospel they had received was truth. I believe the words, *but give you occasion to glory on our behalf,* in this verse supports my opinion.

13 For whether we be beside ourselves, it is to God: or whether we be sober, it is for your cause.

Adam Clarke viewed this verse as saying:
"Beside ourselves - Probably he was reputed by some to be deranged. Festus thought so: *Paul, thou art beside thyself; too much learning hath made thee mad*. And his enemies at Corinth might insinuate not only that he was deranged, but attribute his derangement to a less worthy cause than intense study and deep learning.

Faultfinders search for imperfections, however finite, for faults create schisms. Success for good and for God bother the devil far less than does the absence of fault-finding in a church. There definitely were fault-finding detractors in the Corinthian church, and they seemingly grasped every opportunity to criticize Paul.

I believe the message that Paul intended the words, *whether we be beside ourselves, it is to God: or whether we be sober, it is for your cause,* could be worded: "Don't worry about what they say. What we do, act, or say matters not at all. Our ministry is for you, never for them."

F.B. Meyer lends the following about verse 14:
"It was of small importance in Paul's eyes what his critics thought of him. He desired only to please his supreme Lord, whether he lived or died, was considered cold and staid or hot and impassioned. He was overmastered by his love of Christ. This may have been the sense of Christ's love to his unworthy self, or the emotion that burned in his soul toward Christ, or the very love of Christ received into his heart, as a tiny creek on the shore receives the pulse of the ocean tide."

14 For the love of Christ constraineth us; because we thus judge, that if one died for all, then were all dead:

Greek for "constrain" implies *to compress forcibly* energies into one channel. We are forced to understand that since Christ died for everyone, and He certainly did, then everyone was and is dead in sin without Him. How foolish it would be to pay a debt if no debt existed. It is impossible to pen words that adequately describe the Love of God.

...because we thus judge- We decide; we arrive at a conclusion.

15 And that he died for all, that they which live should not henceforth live unto themselves, but unto him which died for them, and rose again.

All people are given the choice to either accept or reject the propitiation, the death of Jesus Christ, for their sin or reject it. The expression, "I'll do as I please." can never be true. God gives mankind the privilege as to which master to choose—Jesus Christ or the devil. *For ye are bought with a price: therefore, glorify God in your body, and in your spirit, which are God's* (1Cor. 6:20). To surrender to Jesus is to embrace peace and glory. If that is rejected by any, he or she automatically becomes slaves of the devil.

16 ¶ Wherefore henceforth know we no man after the flesh: yea, though we have known Christ after the flesh, yet now henceforth know we him no more,

May we invert this Scripture to read: *though we have known Christ after the flesh, yet now henceforth know we him no more, henceforth know we no man after the flesh.*

...we have known Christ after the flesh, yet now henceforth know we him no more. He walked, talked, hungered and slept like a mortal man, but He is no longer among us in a human form. *Henceforth—*"from this time onward". He has ascended to glory and reigns as the king of kings and Lord of lords.

...know we no man after the flesh- that is, not since the death, burial, and resurrection of Jesus Christ. Nobility, riches, station in

life, etc., matter not at all in salvation's plan. Riches won't buy an entrance into heaven, nor will poverty prevent it if the poor person commits his/her soul to God.

17 Therefore if any man be in Christ, he is a new creature: old things are passed away; behold, all things are become new.

To everyone; young, old, rich, poor, blind, sighted, powerful or weak; the promise is the same: To surrender our souls to the will of God and be born again of water and of the Spirit results in becoming a completely different person.

18 And all things are of God, who hath reconciled us to himself by Jesus Christ, and hath given to us the ministry of reconciliation;

In checking several references for opinions on the 2 words, all things, I found some interesting opinions. I include my own opinion after these distinguished scholars.

Albert T. Barnes: "This refers particularly to the things in question, the renewing of the heart, and the influences by which Paul had been brought to a state of willingness to forsake all, and to devote his life to the self-denying labors involved in the purpose of making the Saviour known."

Adam Clarke: "And all things are of God - As the thorough conversion of the soul is compared to a new creation, and creation is the proper work of an all-wise, almighty Being; then this total change of heart, soul, and life, which takes place under the preaching of the Gospel, is effected by the power and grace of God:"

Jamieson-Fausset-Brown: "all — *Greek,* "THE." things — all our privileges in this new creation."

I believe all 3 comments on this verse zone in on the consequences rather than on the Subject, God. It is God from which all things come into existence. Genesis 1:1 tells us: *In the beginning God created the heaven and the earth.* John 1:3: *All things were made by him; and without him was not anything made that was made.* Colossians 1:16: *For by him were all things created, that are in heaven, and that are in earth, visible and invisible, whether they be thrones, or dominions, or principalities, or powers: all things were created by him, and for him:*

There are 3 things to be considered in verse 18: God-reconciled-reconciliation: Without God, there would be nothing; without God in Christ we could not be reconciled, without God in Christ Jesus, we could not have a ministry of reconciliation.

Reconciliation is defined as: "to be restored to a former state of harmony". However, all people are birthed by their mothers into a state of disharmony—aliens to the God Who created them. Romans 5:14 describes that state: *But not as the offence, so also is the free gift. For if through the offence of one many be dead, much more the grace of God, and the gift by grace, which is by one man, Jesus Christ, hath abounded unto many.* It was no small thing to Paul to pen the words, *hath given to us the ministry of reconciliation;*
19 To wit, that God was in Christ, reconciling the world unto himself, not imputing their trespasses unto them; and hath committed unto us the word of reconciliation.

20 Now then we are ambassadors for Christ, as though God did beseech you by us: we pray you in Christ's stead, be ye reconciled to God.

An ambassador is a person that represents an authoritative person or government. It is a position of great honor. Ambassadors present the requests and/or demands of the person or government that sent them A rearrangement of this verse, as in the following, might be helpful. *...as though God did beseech you...by us...we are ambassadors for Christ...in Christ's stead...we pray you...be ye reconciled to God...*

21 For he hath made him to be sin for us, who knew no sin; that we might be made the righteousness of God in him.

A sinless Jesus Christ accepted the curse of sin to be placed upon Himself. He accepted the curse and died because of it. But He rose from death, having triumphed over the curse of death and hell. As the Eternal, Almighty Savior of men, He beckons: *Come unto me, all ye that labour and are heavy laden, and I will give you rest* (Matthew 11:28).

Bob Koonce Th. D.

CHAPTER SIX

1 We then, as workers together with him, beseech you also that ye receive not the grace of God in vain.

2 (For he saith, I have heard thee in a time accepted, and in the day of salvation have I succoured thee: behold, now is the accepted time; behold, now is the day of salvation.)

3 Giving no offence in any thing, that the ministry be not blamed:

4 But in all things approving ourselves as the ministers of God, in much patience, in afflictions, in necessities, in distresses,

5 In stripes, in imprisonments, in tumults, in labours, in watchings, in fastings;

6 By pureness, by knowledge, by longsuffering, by kindness, by the Holy Ghost, by love unfeigned,

7 By the word of truth, by the power of God, by the armour of righteousness on the right hand and on the left,

8 By honour and dishonour, by evil report and good report: as deceivers, and yet true;

9 As unknown, and yet well known; as dying, and, behold, we live; as chastened, and not killed;

10 As sorrowful, yet alway rejoicing; as poor, yet making many rich; as having nothing, and yet possessing all things.

11 ¶ O ye Corinthians, our mouth is open unto you, our heart is enlarged.

12 Ye are not straitened in us, but ye are straitened in your own bowels.

13 Now for a recompence in the same, (I speak as unto my children,) be ye also enlarged.

14 Be ye not unequally yoked together with unbelievers: for what fellowship hath righteousness with unrighteousness? and what communion hath light with darkness?

15 And what concord hath Christ with Belial? or what part hath he that believeth with an infidel?

16 And what agreement hath the temple of God with idols? for ye are the temple of the living God; as God hath said, I will dwell in them, and walk in them; and I will be their God, and they shall be my people.

17 Wherefore come out from among them, and be ye separate, saith the Lord, and touch not the unclean thing; and I will receive you,

18 And will be a Father unto you, and ye shall be my sons and daughters, saith the Lord Almighty.

In these verses we have an account of the Apostle's general errand and exhortation to all to whom he preached in every place where he came, with the several arguments and methods he used. (Matthew Henry).

"This chapter wrongly isolated at both ends by the customary division of the book. Connection quite closely continuous between 2 Cor. 5:20-21 and 2 Cor. 6:1; as also between 2 Cor. 6:17-18 and 2 Cor. 7:1." (Preacher's Homiletical).

Imperfection in placing verses and Scriptures in perfect order does cause difficulty at times, but a careful reader will endeavor to connect thought to correlating thought. Paul spoke of "rightly dividing the word of truth." The Scriptures to which Paul referred had not at that time been divided into chapters and verses. Still, Paul advised a careful, concerted effort needs to be extended to correctly understand the Word of God.

1 We then, as workers together with him, beseech you also that ye receive not the grace of God in vain.

The words, we then, were added to older texts, but that is of little consequence to the sense of the sentence. The verse could read, "Since we are workers together," and the meaning would be the same. In essence, Paul conveyed the thought, "Since you're going to work with me, I want you to be thoroughly convinced that by the grace of God only can a sinner be saved. We can do nothing apart from the grace of God. It is the grace of God that enables us to win, and it is His grace that sustains us during trials and tribulation."

2 (For he saith, I have heard thee in a time accepted, and in the day of salvation have I succoured thee: behold, now is the accepted time; behold, now is the day of salvation.)

Jamieson-Fausset-Brown gives the following comment on this verse:
"His apostolic ministry is approved by faithfulness in exhortation, in sufferings, in exhibition of the fruits of the Holy Ghost: His largeness of heart to them calls for enlargement of their heart to him.

3 Giving no offence in any thing, that the ministry be not blamed:

"Giving no offense - The word προσκοπη, read προσκομμα, Rom. 14:13, signifies a stumbling block in general, or any thing over which a man stumbles or falls; and here means any transgression or scandal that might take place among the ministers, or the Christians themselves, whereby either Jews or Gentiles might take occasion of offense, and vilify the Gospel of Christ." (Clarke)

4 But in all things approving ourselves as the ministers of God, in much patience, in afflictions, in necessities, in distresses,

A coccineous minister may be subjected to great indignities. He is a target of the devil, thus he also becomes a target for the devil's peons. Mockings, laughter, derisions etc. attack him. He may be denied common courtesies afforded to everyone else, but he refrains from reprisal-verbal or physical. He may be physically harmed, members of his family abused, and so many other cruel things—but he suffers it all for the cause of Christ.

As per Paul's listing, the servant of God may suffer any of the following abuses listed in verses 5-10—and he/she must endure it without giving offence. All this could not be endured without the grace of God.

5 In stripes, in imprisonments, in tumults, in labours, in watchings, in fastings;

- In stripes: Paul and Silas could have given a first-hand report if being whipped nearly to death at Philippi.
- In imprisonments: At midnight in a jail at Philippi, 2 cruelly beaten preachers began to sing! Amazing! The

jailer and his whole family became Christians because of Paul and Silas' faith.
- In tumults: Physical and spiritual. Early Christians' lives were almost constantly endangered; their properties and possessions often seized.
- In labors: Paul was a tent maker by trade. He labored at one time with Aquila and Priscilla, and it was probably he that effected a church in their house.
- In watchings: This surely must imply more than a prayer vigil. A Christian's life was nearly always in danger, whether at home or in public. A constant vigil was always necessary.
- In fastings: So necessary for both body and soul.

The greater part of verse 5 lists cruelties that Christians may individually endure—but the last four words of the verse tells, in part, how to endure them—by fasting and by prayer (watching).

Beginning with verse 6, Paul's focus shifted from the sufferings Christians were then enduring to the subject of how and why the message of Christ had prevailed.

6 By pureness, by knowledge, by longsuffering, by kindness, by the Holy Ghost, by love unfeigned,

By pureness: Jesus said, *"Blessed are the pure in heart: for they shall see God."* (Matthew 5:8)

By knowledge: *Therefore they that were scattered abroad went ever where preaching the word. (*Acts 8:4) Romans 10:14 adds: *How then shall they call on him in whom they have not believed? and how shall they believe in him of whom they have not heard? and how shall they hear without a preacher?* People received knowledge of salvation when they heard the preaching, teaching of the Word of God.

7 By the word of truth, by the power of God, by the armour of righteousness on the right hand and on the left,

The JFB commentary renders the word "by" as "in", making the first phrase of verse 7 to read, "In the word of truth." Fausset's application appears in at least 2 scriptural passages:

For this cause have I sent unto you Timotheus, who is my beloved son, and faithful in the Lord, who shall bring you into remembrance of my ways which be in Christ, as I teach every where in every church (1Cor. 4:17).

Therefore, if any man be in Christ, he is a new creature: old things are passed away; behold, all things are become new (2Cor. 5:17).

By the word of truth: Jesus said: *I am the way, the truth, and the life: no man cometh unto the Father, but by me* (John 14:6). Paul wrote: *But though we, or an angel from heaven, preach any other gospel unto you than that which we have preached unto you, let him be accursed* (Gal. 1:8).

8 By honour and dishonour, by evil report and good report: as deceivers, and yet true;

I present here expositions from Adam Clarke on the key words in this verse. In parenthesis, ( ), I define the more difficult words.

By honor and dishonor: By going through both--sometimes respected, sometimes despised.
By evil report and good report: Sometimes praised, at other times calumniated (lies intended to ruin persons' reputation).
As deceivers: Said to carry about a false doctrine for our secular emolument (compensation).
And yet true: Demonstrated by the nature of the doctrine, as well as by our life and conversation, that we are true men; having nothing in view but God's glory and the salvation of the world.

9 As unknown, and yet well known; as dying, and, behold, we live;
As unknown, and yet well known: "They didn't know us when we first came; they know us well by now." The main intent here is, "Thought men didn't know us, God knew us well."

...as dying, and, behold, we live: In every place where Jesus Christ was preached, arrest, beating, and death lurked for the preacher. Paul flaunted death in the words, *O death, where is thy sting? O grave, where is thy victory? (*1Cor. 15:55). Christians do indeed resist death, as well as do all living things, but they do not fear the hereafter. Death loses its sting in the presence of Jesus Christ!

10 As sorrowful, yet alway rejoicing; as poor, yet making many rich; as having nothing, and yet possessing all things.

As sorrowful, yet alway rejoicing: Jesus said: *Blessed are ye that weep now: for ye shall laugh* (Luke 6:21). *...weeping may endure for a night, but joy cometh in the morning* (Psalm 3:1).
...yet alway rejoicing can be understood in the words: *Looking for that blessed hope, and the glorious appearing of the great God and our Saviour Jesus Christ*; (Titus 2:13)
...as having nothing, and yet possessing all things. In 1Cor. 3:21, Paul penned: *Therefore, let no man glory in men. For <u>all</u> things are <u>yours</u>;* And in 1Timothy 6:7, he wrote: *For we brought nothing into this world, and it is certain we can carry nothing out.*

11 O ye Corinthians, our mouth is open unto you, our heart is enlarged.

O ye Corinthians... Such passionate love for the Corinthians flowed from the point of Paul's pen!

These words addressed the Corinthian church, but not to that church exclusively. There were no Christians in Corinth prior to Paul's arrival there. Paul was the apostle, the sent one, that won converts from heathenism to God in that city. Despite all this, however, there were rebels in the Corinthian congregation. Paul's soul pours forth in the words, *O ye Corinthians*—the faithful; the rebels; the heathens in the city-- *O ye Corinthians!*

...our mouth is open unto you: We yearn to speak to you; to comfort you; to advise you; to help you.
...our heart is enlarged: As the number of believers increases, so does our heart enlarge to embrace the new ones. The longer we

know you, the more affectionate we become of you—our love, our heart has gotten bigger for you.

12 Ye are not straitened in us, but ye are straitened in your own bowels.

Ye are not straitened in us: We love you no less.
...but ye are straitened in your own bowels. You have established limits on your love for us.

13 Now for a recompence in the same, (I speak as unto my children,) be ye also enlarged.

"Now for a recompence in the same – 'By way of recompence, open your hearts in the same manner toward me as I have done toward you. It is all the reward or compensation which I ask of you; all the return which I desire. I do not ask silver or gold, or any earthly possessions. I ask only a return of love, and a devotedness to the cause which I love, and which I endeavor to promote."

"I speak as unto my children - I speak as a parent addressing his children. I sustain toward you the relation of a spiritual father, and I have a right to require and expect a return of affection.

"Be ye also enlarged - Be not straitened in your affections. Love me as I love you. Give to me the same proofs of attachment which I have given you. The idea in this verse is, that the only compensation or remuneration which he expected for all the love which he had shown them, and for all his toils and self-denials in their behalf." (Barnes)

14 Be ye not unequally yoked together with unbelievers: for what fellowship hath righteousness with unrighteousness? and what communion hath light with darkness?

The city of Corinth was filled with the worship of heathen gods. By the power of God, and through the ministry of Paul, heathen worshippers had been converted to Christianity. However, *"...your adversary the devil, as a roaring lion, walketh about, seeking whom he may devour:"* Peter wrote in 1 Peter 5:8. Satan had no intention of permanently surrendering the souls of the Christian converts in Corinth. His plan to win them again? Intermarry his converts with Christians. Very sly indeed!

"Be ye not unequally yoked together with unbelievers - This is a military term: keep in your own ranks; do not leave the Christian community to join in that of the heathens. The verb ἑτεροζυγειν signifies to leave one's own rank, place, or order, and go into another; and here it must signify not only that they should not associate with the Gentiles in their idolatrous feasts, but that they should not apostatize from Christianity;" (Clarke)

"unequally yoked — 'yoked with one alien in spirit.' The image is from the symbolical precept of the law (Lev. 19:19), 'Thou shalt not let thy cattle gender with a diverse kind'; or the precept (Deut. 22:10), 'Thou shalt not plough with an ox and an ass together.'" (Jamieson-Fausset-Brown)

In the Gospel of John, we read: *And the light shineth in darkness; and the darkness comprehended it not.* (John 1:5) White and black mixed together will not produce a true color of either. White will lose its brightness of color-it will become gray. No Christian can give 100% of his/herself and still give God the same amount. Truth and lie cannot cohabit.

15 And what concord hath Christ with Belial? or what part hath he that believeth with an infidel?

There can be no affinity of Christ with Belial (the devil), nor between a saint and an infidel. Jesus Christ is the Master, the Lord of all, of everything that exists. Jesus described Satan as a liar, a deceiver, a thief, and a destroyer. In the wildest of imaginations, how could peace (Jesus) and torment (Satan) dwell in the same mind and soul?

16 And what agreement hath the temple of God with idols? for ye are the temple of the living God; as God hath said, I will dwell in them, and walk in them; and I will be their God, and they shall be my people.

17 Wherefore come out from among them, and be ye separate, saith the Lord, and touch not the unclean thing; and I will receive you,

It is impossible to intermix heavenly things with earthly pleasures. Jesus said to Pilate: *My kingdom is not of this world: if my kingdom were of this world, then would my servants fight..."* (Joh 18:36). 1John 2:15 gives the words: *Love not the world, neither the things that are in the world. If any man love the world, the love of the Father is not in him.*

18 And will be a Father unto you, and ye shall be my sons and daughters, saith the Lord Almighty.

What better Father could there ever be than God Himself?

Fear thou not; for I am with thee: be not dismayed; for I am thy God: I will strengthen thee; yea, I will help thee; yea, I will uphold thee with the right hand of my righteousness (Isaiah 41:10).

Bob Koonce Th. D.

CHAPTER SEVEN

1 Having therefore these promises, dearly beloved, let us cleanse ourselves from all filthiness of the flesh and spirit, perfecting holiness in the fear of God.

2 Receive us; we have wronged no man, we have corrupted no man, we have defrauded no man.

3 I speak not this to condemn you: for I have said before, that ye are in our hearts to die and live with you.

4 Great is my boldness of speech toward you, great is my glorying of you: I am filled with comfort, I am exceeding joyful in all our tribulation.

5 For, when we were come into Macedonia, our flesh had no rest, but we were troubled on every side; without were fightings, within were fears.

6 Nevertheless God, that comforteth those that are cast down, comforted us by the coming of Titus;

7 And not by his coming only, but by the consolation wherewith he was comforted in you, when he told us your earnest desire, your mourning, your fervent mind toward me; so that I rejoiced the more.

8 For though I made you sorry with a letter, I do not repent, though I did repent: for I perceive that the same epistle hath made you sorry, though it were but for a season.

9 Now I rejoice, not that ye were made sorry, but that ye sorrowed to repentance: for ye were made sorry after a godly manner, that ye might receive damage by us in nothing.

10 For godly sorrow worketh repentance to salvation not to be repented of: but the sorrow of the world worketh death.

11 For behold this selfsame thing, that ye sorrowed after a godly sort, what carefulness it wrought in you, yea, what clearing of yourselves, yea, what indignation, yea, what fear, yea, what vehement desire, yea, what zeal, yea, what revenge! In all things ye have approved yourselves to be clear in this matter.

12 Wherefore, though I wrote unto you, I did it not for his cause that had done the wrong, nor for his cause that suffered wrong, but that our care for you in the sight of God might appear unto you.

13 Therefore we were comforted in your comfort: yea, and exceedingly the more joyed we for the joy of Titus, because his spirit was refreshed by you all.
14 For if I have boasted any thing to him of you, I am not ashamed; but as we spake all things to you in truth, even so our boasting, which I made before Titus, is found a truth.
15 And his inward affection is more abundant toward you, whilst he remembereth the obedience of you all, how with fear and trembling ye received him.
16 I rejoice therefore that I have confidence in you in all things.

There seems to be a gap between verse 18 of the previous chapter and the first verse of chapter 7. What can be a bridge between chapter 6:18; "*And will be a Father unto you, and ye shall be my sons and daughters, saith the Lord Almighty,*" and chapter *7:1: "Having therefore these promises, dearly beloved"*?

1 Having therefore these promises, dearly beloved, let us cleanse ourselves from all filthiness of the flesh and spirit, perfecting holiness in the fear of God.

Of the 6 commentaries that I consulted; all approached this chapter with a guess as to which promises Paul intended. I am of the opinion that all of Paul's correspondence to the church of Corinth has not been preserved.

In I Corinthians 12:14, Paul wrote that he was ready to come the third time. In II Corinthians 13:1, he wrote that he was coming the third time. Some speculation exists as to whether the "comings" refer to his visits or to his letters. The only mode of travel was by animal or on foot, and the slowness of either method leads me to believe that some of Paul's letters have not been preserved. And if that truly is the case, the promises he mentioned in verse 1 of this chapter may refer to another letter altogether.

2 Receive us; we have wronged no man, we have corrupted no man, we have defrauded no man.

At first reading of this verse, it appears that Paul inserted "a bump in the road". What relationship can his defense of himself and those with them in this verse have with *"these promises"* of verse 1? However, that application may be amiss. Paul was actually saying, "View us as true, uncorrupted servants of Jesus Christ; love us as such, cease resisting us, and allow us into your hearts to advise and lead you."

"Receive us - Χωρησατε ἡμας. This address is variously understood. Receive us into your affections - love us as we love you. Receive us as your apostles and teachers; we have given you full proof that God hath both sent and owned us. Receive, comprehend, what we now say to you, and carefully mark it." (Clarke)

"Receive us - Tyndale renders this: "understand us." The word used here (χωρησατε chorēsate) means properly, give space, place, or room; and it means here evidently, make place or room for us in your affections; that is, admit or receive us as your friends. It is an earnest entreaty that they would do what he had exhorted them to do in 2Cor. 6:13. From that he had digressed in the close of the last chapter. He here returns to the subject and asks an interest in their affections and their love." (Barnes)

3 I speak not this to condemn you: for I have said before, that ye are in our hearts to die and live with you.

Envision a situation where the greater part of an audience supported you and your values, yet hacklers lurked in the assemblage. They intend to disrupt. They nitpick everything you say or write. Imagine that only the chosen speaker or author is equipped to present a message that hecklers can't spoil. Such was the situation with Paul here. His words in this verse could be worded thus: "We love you sincerely, so please don't think we're condemning you."

4 Great is my boldness of speech toward you, great is my glorying of you: I am filled with comfort, I am exceeding joyful in all our tribulation.

Paul and those with him preached boldly, though they could have been afraid for their lives as they preached. But they prevailed! Conversions from heathenism to Jesus Christ through their ministry naturally thrilled (gloried) Paul and his company. In the midst of their tribulations, they received joy, realizing that Jesus Christ had enabled them to succeed in winning lost souls. One noted commentator expressed the opinion that he though Paul may have inserted this verse to mollify those who may have taken offense over his previous statement in verse 2. I think that is very doubtful. My comment on verse 5 will further explain my reasoning.

5 For, when we were come into Macedonia, our flesh had no rest, but we were troubled on every side; without were fightings, within were fears.

I once heard the expression, "I felt so low that I had to look up to see the bottom!" That's pretty low! It is absolutely terrible to live in a condition where everything bad that could happen does happen. Paul and Titus had barely started witnessing for Jesus Christ at Philippi, their first stop in Macedonia, when they found themselves abused by a crowd, whipped unmercifully, and thrown into the darkest corner of a jail. In Macedonia, plans were laid to kill Paul to the extent that the disciples resorted to a ruse to deceive his intended executioners.

There was no rest in Macedonia. By day, Paul fought the minds and intents of those who wished to silence him; to kill him if possible. At night, there was no satisfactory rest, due to the exhaustion of the day just finished, and apprehension for the next day that was to come.

"our flesh had no rest; that is, their outward man, their bodies; they were continually fatigued with preaching, disputing, fighting; what with false teachers, and violent persecutors, they had no rest in their bodies; though, in their souls, they had divine support and spiritual consolation;" (Gill)

6 Nevertheless God, that comforteth those that are cast down, comforted us by the coming of Titus;

God, that comforteth those that are cast down... Paul made little effort to hide his disappointment and dejection over not meeting Titus as planned. He had felt cast down, and he needed comfort. God provided the comfort he needed in the way he needed it by the arrival of Titus.

Paul had journeyed to Troas to meet Titus, but not finding him, he returned to Macedonia to seek him. Paul was human, and despite the greatness of his character and his resolute intention to preach Christ at every opportunity, the Apostle was not absent of human feelings. He needed Titus; he needed the scrolls that Titus was to bring; finding neither Titus nor the scrolls deeply affected Paul. How happy he must have been when Titus eventually appeared.

7 And not by his coming only, but by the consolation wherewith he was comforted in you, when he told us your earnest desire, your mourning, your fervent mind toward me; so that I rejoiced the more.

The joy and comfort that Paul felt at Titus' return was not limited to their reunion. Titus came with an uplifting report concerning the congregation at Corinth. Paul was overjoyed.

The Popular New Testament adds the following words concerning Titus' coming: "and not by his coming only, but also by the comfort wherewith he was comforted in you—bringing back such gladdening intelligence of your spiritual state,—when he told us your longing—to see me again,—your mourning, your zeal for me—in spite of malicious insinuation against me,—so that I rejoiced yet more—than at his mere return."

8 For though I made you sorry with a letter, I do not repent, though I did repent: for I perceive that the same epistle hath made you sorry, though it were but for a season.

As a loving parent in I Corinthians, chapter 6, Paul scolded the Corinthian church for allowing lawsuits of brother against brother in civil court. No matter how much parents love their children, they realize that they must be corrected at times. Correction time is never pleasant, but it is necessary to keep children on course. So, also, it is with children of God. They are God's children, but they won't reach perfection until they find themselves in heaven. Until then,

God furnishes them with *apostles; and some, prophets; and some, evangelists; and some, pastors and teachers;* ¹² *For the perfecting of the saints, for the work of the ministry, for the edifying of the body of Christ:* (Ephesians 4:11-12)

9 Now I rejoice, not that ye were made sorry, but that ye sorrowed to repentance: for ye were made sorry after a godly manner, that ye might receive damage by us in nothing.
10 For godly sorrow worketh repentance to salvation not to be repented of: but the sorrow of the world worketh death.

It is easy to become confused about the reason for Paul's scolding the church at Corinth. It is often explained that the subject Paul addressed in the letter to which he here referred, addressed the incestuous fornicator in that church. Verse 12 of this chapter tells us that the fornicator was not that subject at all. He referred to lawsuits of brother against brother in civil court in this instance.

11 For behold this selfsame thing, that ye sorrowed after a godly sort, what carefulness it wrought in you, yea, what clearing of yourselves, yea, what indignation, yea, what fear, yea, what vehement desire, yea, what zeal, yea, what revenge! In all things ye have approved yourselves to be clear in this matter.

In this verse, Paul was not endorsing nor urging violence. He wrote, *ye sorrowed after a godly sort.* Merriam-Webster explains vehement as "strong, powerful". Paul was pleased that the church unapologetically corrected the problem powerfully-vehemently.

12 Wherefore, though I wrote unto you, I did it not for his cause that had done the wrong, nor for his cause that suffered wrong, but that our care for you in the sight of God might appear unto you.

1Cor. 6:6 *But brother goeth to law with brother, and that before the unbelievers.* This situation prompted a scolding from Paul in his first epistle to the church. Titus came from Corinth with news for Paul that the church had corrected the problem.

13 Therefore we were comforted in your comfort: yea, and exceedingly the more joyed we for the joy of Titus, because his spirit was refreshed by you all.

"Therefore, we were comforted in your comfort - The phrase 'your comfort,' here seems to mean the happiness which they had, or might reasonably be expected to have in obeying the directions of Paul, and in the repentance which they had manifested. Paul had spoken of no other consolation or comfort than this; and the idea seems to be that they were a happy people and would be happy by obeying the commands of God. This fact gave Paul additional joy, and he could not but rejoice that they had removed the cause of the offence, and that they would not thus be exposed to the displeasure of God. Had they not repented and put away the evil, the consequences to them must have been deep distress. As it was, they would be blessed and happy." (Barnes)

14 For if I have boasted any thing to him of you, I am not ashamed; but as we spake all things to you in truth, even so our boasting, which I made before Titus, is found a truth.

The word, boasting, certainly is not applicable for Paul. In Romans 3:27, he wrote: *Where is boasting then? It is excluded. By what law? of works? Nay: but by the law of faith.* Boasting by Paul must be understood as "commendation" or "approval". He wrote that he was not ashamed (not embarrassed) for any of the commendations he had given for the Corinthian saints.

"For if I have boasted - The apostle had given Titus a very high character of this Church, and of their attachment to himself; and doubtless this was the case previously to the evil teacher getting among them, who had succeeded in changing their conduct, and changing in a great measure their character also; but now they return to themselves, resume their lost ground, so that the good character which the apostle gave them before, and which they had for a time forfeited, is now as applicable to them as ever. Therefore, his boasting of them is still found a truth." (Clarke)

15 And his inward affection is more abundant toward you, whilst he remembereth the obedience of you all, how with fear and trembling ye received him.

The subject here is Titus who had learned to love the Corinthian saints more abundantly after visiting them personally. He learned that Paul's endorsement of them had not been misplaced

"how with fear and trembling you received him; that is, with great humility and respect, with much deference to him: considering his character as a minister of the Gospel, and as one sent by the apostle to them, they embraced him with great marks of honour and esteem; for this is not to be understood of any inward slavish fear or dread of mind, or trembling of body at the sight of him, and because he came to know their estate, and with reproofs from the apostle to them." (Gill)

Several commentaries offer the same interpretation for fear and trembling as did Gill. I am not qualified to refute that interpretation, nor do I intend to. It could be entirely correct, and while I agree with reservations, I think there is more to be considered in discussing fear and trembling.

Christians were despised by the heathen worshippers among whom they lived. Barbaric acts were inflicted upon them; they were beaten, tortured, stoned and killed. They were spied upon, and a new arrival among them would have been immediately noticed by those that hated them. They lived in danger, existed in fear, expecting evil at every turn. It is my opinion that they received Titus' arrival with apprehension—with fear and trembling.

16 I rejoice therefore that I have confidence in you in all things.

How truly wonderful it is for anxiety to be put to rest. Titus assured Paul of the Corinthians' faith, obedience to Scriptural instruction and, importantly, their great love for him.

CHAPTER EIGHT

1 *Moreover, brethren, we do you to wit of the grace of God bestowed on the churches of Macedonia;*
2 How that in a great trial of affliction the abundance of their joy and their deep poverty abounded unto the riches of their liberality.
3 For to their power, I bear record, yea, and beyond their power they were willing of themselves;
4 Praying us with much intreaty that we would receive the gift, and take upon us the fellowship of the ministering to the saints.
5 And this they did, not as we hoped, but first gave their own selves to the Lord, and unto us by the will of God.
6 Insomuch that we desired Titus, that as he had begun, so he would also finish in you the same grace also.
7 ¶ Therefore, as ye abound in every thing, in faith, and utterance, and knowledge, and in all diligence, and in your love to us, see that ye abound in this grace also.
8 I speak not by commandment, but by occasion of the forwardness of others, and to prove the sincerity of your love.
9 For ye know the grace of our Lord Jesus Christ, that, though he was rich, yet for your sakes he became poor, that ye through his poverty might be rich.
10 And herein I give my advice: for this is expedient for you, who have begun before, not only to do, but also to be forward a year ago.
11 Now therefore perform the doing of it; that as there was a readiness to will, so there may be a performance also out of that which ye have.
12 For if there be first a willing mind, it is accepted according to that a man hath, and not according to that he hath not.
13 For I mean not that other men be eased, and ye burdened:
14 But by an equality, that now at this time your abundance may be a supply for their want, that their abundance also may be a supply for your want: that there may be equality:
15 As it is written, He that had gathered much had nothing over; and he that had gathered little had no lack.
16 ¶ But thanks be to God, which put the same earnest care into

the heart of Titus for you.

17 For indeed he accepted the exhortation; but being more forward, of his own accord he went unto you.

18 And we have sent with him the brother, whose praise is in the gospel throughout all the churches;

19 And not that only, but who was also chosen of the churches to travel with us with this grace, which is administered by us to the glory of the same Lord, and declaration of your ready mind:

20 Avoiding this, that no man should blame us in this abundance which is administered by us:

21 Providing for honest things, not only in the sight of the Lord, but also in the sight of men.

22 And we have sent with them our brother, whom we have oftentimes proved diligent in many things, but now much more diligent, upon the great confidence which I have in you.

23 Whether any do enquire of Titus, he is my partner and fellowhelper concerning you: or our brethren be enquired of, they are the messengers of the churches, and the glory of Christ.

24 Wherefore shew ye to them, and before the churches, the proof of your love, and of our boasting on your behalf.

It could be rightly said that Paul was a great apostle while still attributing other significant credits to him as well. He was well-educated, an education that amazed the Roman governor, Festus. While never a politician, he possessed a power of persuasion that any politician would envy. He was a diplomat; he was able to scold his converts when the need arose, but he scolded as a father would. True Christians received and repented when reprimanded. Dissenters became immediately aware that they had been exposed.

In the last several verses of the preceding chapter, Paul expressed his thanks to the Corinthian church for having received and obeyed his instructions. The Apostle's ministry never ceased. He introduced a new subject, a new need, in the opening verses of Chapter 8.

1 Moreover, brethren, we do you to wit of the grace of God bestowed on the churches of Macedonia;

Moreover… A word used here to convey the thought that what he had written was leading to something he was about to introduce. He had commended the Corinth church for their obedience, generosity, etc., and not for selfish purpose. However, the need to inform the saints there that their generosity and love for him was not unmatched, but was matched by the churches at Philippi, Thessalonica, and Berea, and others.

2 How that in a great trial of affliction the abundance of their joy and their deep poverty abounded unto the riches of their liberality.

This verse does not inform believers that God turns poverty into riches and cruel trials of believers' faith into wealth. Prosperity for all believers is so untrue! It was in circumstances of great affliction <u>and</u> in deep poverty (they counted themselves blessed to have food to eat), that they gave so liberally.

"trial of affliction — The *Greek* expresses, 'in affliction (or, 'tribulation') which *tested* them' literally, 'in a great testing of affliction.'" (Jamiesson-Fausset-Brown)

"How that in a great trial of affliction…. The apostle proceeds to show the condition these churches were in when, and the manner in which, they contributed to the relief of others. They were in affliction: they received the Gospel at first in much affliction, as did the church at Thessalonica, which was one of them; and afterwards suffered much from their countrymen for the profession of it, by reproaches, persecutions, imprisonments, confiscation of goods, &c. They were under trying afflictions, which tried their faith and patience." (Gill)

3 For to their power, I bear record, yea, and beyond their power they were willing of themselves;

The Macedonian churches had given everything they could have given and, in giving, they held nothing back. In fact, they left themselves in need in order to give. Paul wrote, "I bear them record, i.e., I vouch for them."

4 Praying us with much entreaty that we would receive the gift, and take upon us the fellowship of the ministering to the saints.

Praying us with much entreaty.... "They pleaded with us." In my mind, I think the hidden meaning for these words is, "We're very sorry that we couldn't have collected more. Forgive us please, and please take the little that we are able to give—please!"

5 And this they did, not as we hoped, but first gave their own selves to the Lord, and unto us by the will of God.

.... not as we hoped.... They gave more than Paul had expected them to give. In a land of plenty, it may be impossible to understand a condition such as was the case in this verse.

6 Insomuch that we desired Titus, that as he had begun, so he would also finish in you the same grace also.

Several commentaries explain this verse to mean that Titus had presented the need for the churches in Jude and had initiated a collection for that need by the Corinthian church. That may be true, were it not for the words, *"he would also finish in you the same grace also."* These last few words in verse 6 lead me to believe that Paul had desired Titus to further teach and train the Corinthians in the doctrine that he introduced to them.

In my opinion, I believe that verses 1 and 2 of this chapter were written as a "softening up" of the minds and wills of the Corinthians. Most Christians in the heathen world suffered needs. The Corinthians could have been somewhat dismayed upon receiving a request to give more when they may have possessed barely enough to meet their own needs. So, rather that approach them bluntly, Paul cited the liberality of the other Macedonian churches. The Corinthians could hardly ignore the need of the destitute Christians in Judea when the other churches in Macedonia had responded readily and sacrificially.

7 Therefore, as ye abound in everything, in faith, and utterance, and knowledge, and in all diligence, and in your love to us, see that ye abound in this grace also.
Abound: To be present in large numbers or quality (Merriam

Webster Collegiate Dictionary). Paul here linked abounding with grace-- *see that ye abound in this grace also.* He was not expecting a token offering; he prayed for a bountiful response. It seems that Paul was urging the Corinthians to respond to the need with a zeal equal to the zeal with which they pursued the gifts of the Spirt, coupled with the fruit of the Spirit—love, joy, peace, longsuffering, faith, meekness, and temperance.

As ye abound in every thing - In faith, crediting the whole testimony of God; in utterance, λογω, in doctrine, knowing what to teach: knowledge of God's will, and prudence to direct you in teaching and doing it; in diligence, to amend all that is wrong among you, and to do what is right; and in love to us, whom now ye prize as the apostles of the Lord, and your pastors in him. (Clarke)

8 I speak not by commandment, but by occasion of the forwardness of others, and to prove the sincerity of your love.

- *.... not by commandment....* Not quoting from the Mosaic Law.
- *....occasion of the forwardness of others....* In that the other churches have so done.
- *....and to prove the sincerity of your love.* To give you opportunity to share the same blessings as have the other churches who have given so liberally.

But by occasion of the forwardness of others - I make use of the example of the churches of Macedonia as an argument to induce you to give liberally to the cause (Barnes).

9 For ye know the grace of our Lord Jesus Christ, that, though he was rich, yet for your sakes he became poor, that ye through his poverty might be rich.

Paul couldn't have cited a better example of unselfish love and generosity than the Lord Jesus Christ. Jesus came to earth to die, to give everything. Though by Him was all creation made, He put all that aside that He, the Beauty of all Creation, might live and die like a mortal man.

10 And herein I give my advice: for this is expedient for you, who have begun before, not only to do, but also to be forward a year ago.

The need of the churches in Judea is here presented as urgent. Whatever the reason for their dire distress may have been, they desperately needed help. Christians there may have been starving, yet there could well have been another urgent need—but, whatever the need, it was urgent.

It does not appear that the Corinthian Christians were hesitant in responding to the need, but it does seem that at the time of Paul's writing, they had yet to finish the collection started a year prior.

11 Now therefore perform the doing of it; that as there was a readiness to will, so there may be a performance also out of that which ye have.

Now therefore perform.... Good intentions not brought to fruition, are comparable to fruit left unpicked. No one is profited. Paul's words in this verse demonstrates the need for action upon the good intentions the church at Corinth had originally displayed.

12 For if there be first a willing mind, it is accepted according to that a man hath, and not according to that he hath not.

For if there be first a willing mind.... There were slave owners and also slaves in the same congregation in the early churches. This is hard to understand in a free world, but a fact in Paul's period of time. Christian slaves would have possessed willing minds, but they would have had very little to give. On the other hand, slave owners would have been able to give much more to contribute. Whether slave or slave owner, Paul expressed that the giving be done with a willing mind.

13 For I mean not that other men be eased, and ye burdened:

I understand *not that other men be eased* as meaning that wealthy persons were expected to contribute the percentage of their resources to equal the percentage expected of the poor man's resources.

14 But by an equality, that now at this time your abundance may be a supply for their want, that their abundance also may be a supply for your want: that there may be equality:

Subjects are sometimes obscured, sometimes even lost amidst explanations. Corinth is not the subject to which this verse refers. The poor churches in Judea and their urgent plea for aid is the true subject of this discourse. Corinth certainly was a prosperous city during Paul's ministry, and the Apostle did admonish the church there to share more of its bounty. I think it is erroneous, however, to interpret this verse to infer that their liberality was intended to relieve other Macedonian churches. It was intended to relieve the poor saints in Judea.

15 As it is written, He that had gathered much had nothing over; and he that had gathered little had no lack.

Manna (meaning: what is it?) was given for food to the tribes of Israel as they wandered in the wilderness for 40 years. It appeared like frost on the ground each morning. Worms infested manna when too much of it was intentionally gathered, while there was still enough manna to feed a family, even if too little had unintentionally been gathered. The lesson here is not in the action of giving, but of the spirit in which an offering is made.

Barnes' Commentary offers the following on this verse:
"Paul applies this passage, therefore, in the very spirit in which it was originally penned. He means to say that the rich Christians at Corinth should impart freely to their poorer brethren. They had gathered more wealth than was immediately necessary for their families or themselves. They should, therefore, impart freely to those who had been less successful. Wealth, like manna, is the gift of God. It is like that spread by his hand around us every day. Some are able to gather much more than others. By their skill, their health, their diligence, or by providential arrangements, they are eminently successful. Others are feeble, or sick, or aged, or destitute of skill, and are less successful. All that is obtained is by

the arrangement of God. The health, the strength, the skill, the wisdom by which we are enabled to obtain it, are all his gift. That which is thus honestly obtained, therefore, should be regarded as his bounty, and we should esteem it a privilege daily to impart to others less favored and less successful."

16 But thanks be to God, which put the same earnest into the heart of Titus for you.

.... the same earnest.... The word, earnest, carries the connotation of an investment. Paul and Titus, as co-pastors, were of the same spirit and possessed the same love and care for the Corinthian church.

17 For indeed he accepted the exhortation; but being more forward, of his own accord he went unto you.

.... he accepted the exhortation.... According to Merriam-Webster, an exhortation is a language intended to incite and encourage. There must be little doubt that Paul did encourage Titus with all sincerity to go to Corinth. But of Titus' *own accord*, of his own free will, he accepted the challenge. It is very apparent that the 2 men shared the same spirit to help and bless believers.

18 And we have sent with him the brother, whose praise is in the gospel throughout all the churches;
19 And not that only, but who was also chosen of the churches to travel with us with this grace, which is administered by us to the glory of the same Lord, and declaration of your ready mind:

The brother, to whom Paul alludes in this verse, must forever remain a mystery. Some commentators think it to be Silas, some Barnabus, while others think it Mark. Whoever the man, Paul attributed the words, *whose praise is in the gospel throughout all the churches.* The man was well-known by all the existing churches. Yet Paul wrote, *we have sent... the brother.*

I believe there to be a definite break in subjects between verse 18 and verse 19. Verse 18 uses the words, *we have sent* - Paul and company sent them. Paul did not go with them. Verse 19 states, *to travel with us.* That expression informs the reader that the trip with the funds for the poor saints in Judea is here to be understood. With that understanding, verse 20 is more easily understood.

20 Avoiding this, that no man should blame us in this abundance which is administered by us:

...blame us in this abundance... Paul and those with him carried the contributions from all the churches to the Christians in Judea. The Apostle was well aware of the danger that dissenters might accuse him of filching some of the contributions for himself. *Avoiding this*—he had wisely required beforehand that anyone chosen to go with him must be endorsed by the church that recommended him.

21 Providing for honest things, not only in the sight of the Lord, but also in the sight of men.

I Corinthians 16:1-3 shows the precaution Paul took to provide proof for his honesty:
¹ Now concerning the collection for the saints, as I have given order to the churches of Galatia, even so do ye.
² Upon the first day of the week let every one of you lay by him in store, as God hath prospered him, that there be no gatherings when I come.
³ And when I come, whomsoever ye shall approve by your letters, them will I send to bring your liberality unto Jerusalem.

Again, Paul switched subjects. He reverted to verse 16 and the discussion of sending Titus to Corinth with those designated to go with him.

22 And we have sent with them our brother, whom we have oftentimes proved diligent in many things, but now much more diligent, upon the great confidence which I have in you.

...we have sent with them our brother... Though commentators disagree as to whom "brother" refers, I think that Paul's inclusion of Titus' name in verse 23 identifies him as the brother. Paul wrote, *we have oftentimes proved diligent*, indicating that an extended

association between the two had existed before the time of this writing. Had Barnabas, Silas, Timothy, or Mark's name been mentioned in any of these verses, it might be reasonable to think one of them might have been the intended person—but none of those names were mentioned.

23 Whether any do enquire of Titus, he is my partner and fellowhelper concerning you: or our brethren be enquired of, they are the messengers of the churches, and the glory of Christ.

Whether any do enquire of Titus... This phrase so definitely identifies the brother mentioned in the preceding verse. Paul could have started this verse with the words, "If any of the dissenters questions the qualifications of Titus, he is my partner! And the same thing holds true for all the brethren who are my associates."

24 Wherefore shew ye to them, and before the churches, the proof of your love, and of our boasting on your behalf.

Let's rearrange this verse in the following order: *Wherefore* (now) *shew ye before the churches and to them the proof of your love, i.e.* It's time for you to express your love, your allegiance, and your appreciation to all who have done so much for you.

...our boasting on your behalf should not be understood as bragging; rather understood as Paul's confidence in the faithful members of that church.

CHAPTER NINE

1 For as touching the ministering to the saints, it is superfluous for me to write to you:

2 For I know the forwardness of your mind, for which I boast of you to them of Macedonia, that Achaia was ready a year ago; and your zeal hath provoked very many.

3 Yet have I sent the brethren, lest our boasting of you should be in vain in this behalf; that, as I said, ye may be ready:

4 Lest haply if they of Macedonia come with me, and find you unprepared, we (that we say not, ye) should be ashamed in this same confident boasting.

5 Therefore I thought it necessary to exhort the brethren, that they would go before unto you, and make up beforehand your bounty, whereof ye had notice before, that the same might be ready, as a matter of bounty, and not as of covetousness.

6 But this I say, He which soweth sparingly shall reap also sparingly; and he which soweth bountifully shall reap also bountifully.

7 Every man according as he purposeth in his heart, so let him give; not grudgingly, or of necessity: for God loveth a cheerful giver.

8 And God is able to make all grace abound toward you; that ye, always having all sufficiency in all things, may abound to every good work:

9 (As it is written, He hath dispersed abroad; he hath given to the poor: his righteousness remaineth for ever.

10 Now he that ministereth seed to the sower both minister bread for your food, and multiply your seed sown, and increase the fruits of your righteousness;)

11 Being enriched in every thing to all bountifulness, which causeth through us thanksgiving to God.

12 For the administration of this service not only supplieth the want of the saints, but is abundant also by many thanksgivings unto God;

13 Whiles by the experiment of this ministration they glorify God for your professed subjection unto the gospel of Christ, and for your

liberal distribution unto them, and unto all men;
14 And by their prayer for you, which long after you for the exceeding grace of God in you.
15 Thanks be unto God for his unspeakable gift.

I think it very doubtful that II Corinthians is the second of only 2 epistles that Paul penned to the church at Corinth. It definitely is true that only 2 epistles have survived the ravages of time, but that fact alone does not prove that only 2 were ever written. Yet, had there been more instructions for Christians that needed to be preserved, they surely would still be available.

In chapter 8, Paul inserted words of praise for the faithfulness and generosity of the Corinthians. Chapter 9 opens with words of considerable anxiety about the collection at Corinth for the starving saints at Jerusalem. It would be erroneous to think that Paul was concerned for the poor saints in Judea simply because he also was a Jew. It is correct to think that Paul loved all Christians, no matter their race, and constantly promoted unity among all the brethren.

1 For as touching the ministering to the saints, it is superfluous for me to write to you:

Superfluous—not needed, not necessary. This verse seems redundant, yet it has the connotation of "taking a breath between statements." *For as touching the ministering to the saints...* The verse should be reversed to read: *It is superfluous for me to write to you touching the ministering to the saints.* Apparently, the Corinthians responded quickly to needful causes. That definition seems to be the sense of the sentence in verse 2: *Achaia was ready a year ago*

2 For I know the forwardness of your mind, for which I boast of you to them of Macedonia, that Achaia was ready a year ago; and your zeal hath provoked very many.

For I know the forwardness of your mind... the readiness, the promptness. The zeal displayed by the church at Corinth inspired other churches to react in like manner. This clause seems to say, "I know how you respond to a need, but..." Paul appeared to be anxious about whether the Corinthians had completed the collection.

3 Yet have I sent the brethren, lest our boasting of you should be in vain in this behalf; that, as I said, ye may be ready:
4 Lest haply if they of Macedonia come with me, and find you unprepared, we (that we say not, ye) should be ashamed in this same confident boasting.

There was much at stake concerning the Corinthians' response in completing the collection. 1. If the church there had failed to complete the collection by the time of Paul's arrival, it would have destroyed their reputation in other churches. 2. It would have destroyed Paul's faith and trusts in them. 3. It would have made it appear that Paul was no more than a boaster. 4. It would have destroyed faith in Paul in all the other churches.

Paul wrote, *"If they of Macedonia come with me and find you unprepared, we should* (would) *be ashamed."* The Apostle might have questioned his own leadership quality. He thought that more assurance than a letter was needed to ensure that the collection had been completed.

5 Therefore I thought it necessary to exhort the brethren, that they would go before unto you, and make up beforehand your bounty, whereof ye had notice before, that the same might be ready, as a matter of bounty, and not as of covetousness.

Paul was a dedicated apostle, tending matters of ministry carefully and cautiously. He *exhorted* Titus and the other brethren. Careful instructions were given on how to approach the Corinthian brethren concerning the collection. If it had not been completed, Titus and the brethren with him were to tactfully, yet actively become involved in its completion.

I rearrange verse 5 in order to properly explain the phrase *"and not as of covetousness"*.

Therefore I thought it necessary to exhort the brethren, that they would go before unto you, and make up beforehand your bounty, not as of covetousness (not for our own selfish reasons).

...whereof ye had notice before... This was not a rebuke; rather it should be understood as a preparatory statement with the understanding, "The brethren are come to you to help you with the collection for the poor saints that we previously discussed with you."

6 But this I say, He which soweth sparingly shall reap also sparingly; and he which soweth bountifully shall reap also bountifully.

Here again, Paul referred to the Mosaic Law and to the Prophets:
Sow to yourselves in righteousness, reap in mercy; break up your fallow ground: for it is time to seek the LORD, till he come and rain righteousness upon you (Hosea 10:12). It is said that the Jews translated this verse in these words: "Sow to yourselves almsgiving, and ye shall reap in mercy - if you show mercy to the poor, God will show mercy to you." I think that translation is very fitting.

It is a law of the harvest that reaping depends entirely on sowing. No more can be reaped than that which is sown. Put few seeds in the ground—expect harvest from few plants. Sow many seeds—expect an abundant harvest. Give unselfishly—expect an abundant reward.

7 Every man according as he purposeth in his heart, so let him give; not grudgingly, or of necessity: for God loveth a cheerful giver.

...not grudgingly... as something forcefully taken. Something surrendered under pressure is not a gift. It is as though something as been taken and not as though something has been given. A grudging contributor counts what he has left; a cheerful giver counts what he has gained. *God loveth a cheerful giver.*

Clarke's Commentary gives this interpretation for this verse:
"Not grudgingly, or of necessity - The Jews had in the temple two chests for alms; the one was של תובה of what was necessary, i.e. what the law required, the other was של נרבה of the free-will offerings. To escape perdition some would grudgingly give what necessity obliged them; others would give cheerfully, for the love of God, and through pity to the poor. Of the first, nothing is said; they simply did what the law required. Of the second, much is said; God loves them. The benefit of almsgiving is lost to the giver when

he does it with a grumbling heart. And, as he does not do the duty in the spirit of the duty, even the performance of the letter of the law is an abomination in the sight of God. To these two sorts of alms in the temple the apostle most evidently alludes."

8 And God is able to make all grace abound toward you; that ye, always having all sufficiency in all things, may abound to every good work:

And God is able to... What is He not able to? There is nothing He can't do! He makes grace abound, there is always *having all sufficiency in all things.* This phrase is insurance that all assurance from God is inexhaustible eternally.

9 (As it is written, He hath dispersed abroad; he hath given to the poor: his righteousness remaineth for ever.

Paul here inserted Scripture to affirm his statement. I translate this verse as: "He has given of His abundance beyond your borders; He gives to the poor everywhere; there is no end to His righteousness."

10 Now he that ministereth seed to the sower both minister bread for your food, and multiply your seed sown, and increase the fruits of your righteousness;)

God provides seed to the sower to provide food for the sower. He multiplies the harvest as a reward for the sower's righteousness.

11 Being enriched in every thing to all bountifulness, which causeth through us thanksgiving to God.

Being enriched by an abundant harvest causes the sower to thank God for the abundance of the harvest.

12 For the administration of this service not only supplieth the want of the saints, but is abundant also by many thanksgivings unto God;

As Christians respond to the needs of other needy Christians, it causes them to thank God, and it causes the receivers to thank God for the gift, thus many thanksgivings result.

13 Whiles by the experiment of this ministration they glorify God for your professed subjection unto the gospel of Christ, and for your liberal distribution unto them, and unto all men;

Whiles by the experiment (experience) of this ministration.... The poor saints at Jerusalem gained relief through the liberality of the Gentile churches ministered to them by the apostles. They glorified God for the relief and gave thanks to Him

.... *your professed* (your exemplified) *subjection unto the gospel of Christ....* The Jewish believers at Jerusalem were deeply impressed that Gentile Christians had liberally responded to their needs.

14 And by their prayer for you, which long after you for the exceeding grace of God in you.

"They are praying for you; they want to meet you and witness God's amazing grace in you Gentile believers."

The reluctance of Jewish believers to mingle with and accept Gentiles as fellow saints eventually divided the two and led to a permanent division.

15 Thanks be unto God for his unspeakable gift.

Thanks be unto God for his unspeakable gift. Some commentators think this could refer to either the goodness of God, or to the gift itself. I find some difficulty in accepting that the gift is here indicated since the wording describes it as "unspeakable". I view the word to mean "beyond comprehension" and that could hardly describe an earthly gift. In my mind, "unspeakable" surely must refer to John 3:16: *For God so loved the world, that he gave his only begotten Son, that whosoever believeth in him should not perish, but have everlasting life.* This is, without doubt, beyond man's comprehension.

CHAPTER TEN

1 Now I Paul myself beseech you by the meekness and gentleness of Christ, who in presence am base among you, but being absent am bold toward you:

2 But I beseech you, that I may not be bold when I am present with that confidence, wherewith I think to be bold against some, which think of us as if we walked according to the flesh.

3 For though we walk in the flesh, we do not war after the flesh:

4 (For the weapons of our warfare are not carnal, but mighty through God to the pulling down of strong holds;)

5 Casting down imaginations, and every high thing that exalteth itself against the knowledge of God, and bringing into captivity every thought to the obedience of Christ;

6 And having in a readiness to revenge all disobedience, when your obedience is fulfilled.

7 Do ye look on things after the outward appearance? If any man trust to himself that he is Christ's, let him of himself think this again, that, as he is Christ's, even so are we Christ's.

8 For though I should boast somewhat more of our authority, which the Lord hath given us for edification, and not for your destruction, I should not be ashamed:

9 That I may not seem as if I would terrify you by letters.

10 For his letters, say they, are weighty and powerful; but his bodily presence is weak, and his speech contemptible.

11 Let such an one think this, that, such as we are in word by letters when we are absent, such will we be also in deed when we are present.

12 For we dare not make ourselves of the number, or compare ourselves with some that commend themselves: but they measuring themselves by themselves, and comparing themselves among themselves, are not wise.

13 But we will not boast of things without our measure, but according to the measure of the rule which God hath distributed to us, a measure to reach even unto you.

14 For we stretch not ourselves beyond our measure, as though we reached not unto you: for we are come as far as to you also in preaching the gospel of Christ:

15 Not boasting of things without our measure, that is, of other men's labours; but having hope, when your faith is increased, that we shall be enlarged by you according to our rule abundantly,

16 To preach the gospel in the regions beyond you, and not to boast in another man's line of things made ready to our hand.

17 But he that glorieth, let him glory in the Lord.

18 For not he that commendeth himself is approved, but whom the Lord commendeth.

With an unexpected abruptness, Paul's letter changed from a tone of praise for the Corinthian church for its generosity to one of warning again of false teachers within it.

1 Now I Paul myself beseech you by the meekness and gentleness of Christ, who in presence am base among you, but being absent am bold toward you:

I Paul myself beseech you.... As though he were there personally, he *beseeched* (begged) them. Before his conversion, Paul had enjoyed some measure of wealth, was a Roman citizen, and had gained considerable stature among his peers. There was nothing of material gain for him in preaching Christ to the Gentiles. How deeply troubling it must have been for him to continually battle false teachers with their false doctrines within the Church. His use of the word, beseech, seems to convey the thought of some despair. He used the same word again in the following verse.

- *.... who in presence am base....* Humble, as in the words, *by the meekness and gentleness of Christ*
- *.... being absent am bold....* Not apologetic. Commending them with a sense of pride.

2 But I beseech you, that I may not be bold when I am present with that confidence, wherewith I think to be bold against some, which think of us as if we walked according to the flesh.

Rearranged for better understanding, this verse would read:
But when I am present, I beseech you that I may not be bold with that confidence wherewith I think to be bold against some, which

think of us as if we walked according to the flesh. A paraphrase of the verse is: "I am not a coward. I oppose false doctrine and false teachers vehemently. I do not want to come to you with a fighting spirit, except for the false teachers among you."

.... some, which think of us as if we walked according to the flesh.... "As they determine in their own carnal minds and act accordingly, so do they think that we will react like selfish, carnal persons."

3 For though we walk in the flesh, we do not war after the flesh:

"Paul here makes his defense." wrote several commentators. I disagree with the word "defense" in this instance in that Paul attacked the false teachers' doctrine rather than accept being attacked. Some who resisted his authority spoke disparagingly of his body and his ineloquent speech. To their followers, they presented the argumentative question as to why they should yield absolute submission to his words. The dissenters may have gone so far as to suggest that he was nothing other than a schemer.

.... we do not war after the flesh: Christians have always appeared as enigmas to non-Christians. They are not selfish, self-centered, anger slowly and with restraint, suffer abuse patiently, love their enemies, and are patient and kind. Though they are human just as all men are, they do not accept nor practice the immorality of the bulk of humanity. They bless their abusers and pray for their enemies. They do not *war after the flesh.*

Paul described the enemy with which Christians are continually and constantly engaged. Ephesians 6:12: *For we wrestle not against flesh and blood, but against principalities, against powers, against the rulers of the darkness of this world, against spiritual wickedness in high places.*

I find a comment by Barnes on this verse interesting:
"The warfare in which he was engaged was with sin, idolatry, and all forms of evil. He means that in conducting this he was not actuated by worldly views or policy, or by such ambitious and interested aims as controlled the people of this world. This refers

primarily to the warfare in which Paul was himself engaged as an apostle; and the idea is, that he went forth as a soldier under the great Captain of his salvation to fight his battles and to make conquests for him."

4 (For the weapons of our warfare are not carnal, but mighty through God to the pulling down of strong holds;)

.... weapons of our warfare: These are described in Ephesians. 6:14-17:

14 Stand therefore, having your loins girt about with truth, and having on the breastplate of righteousness;
15 And your feet shod with the preparation of the gospel of peace;
16 Above all, taking the shield of faith, wherewith ye shall be able to quench all the fiery darts of the wicked.
17 And take the helmet of salvation, and the sword of the Spirit, which is the word of God:

Weapons are effective only when they are used. But how mighty are they when employed in battle for the Master! Notice the powerful description of that action in the next 2 verses.

5 Casting down imaginations, and every high thing that exalteth itself against the knowledge of God, and bringing into captivity every thought to the obedience of Christ;

Casting down: Violent, determined action like that of casting down the stones of a fortified wall by victors in a war.

Casting down <u>imaginations:</u> In Proverbs 23:7, Solomon wrote: *For as he thinketh in his heart, so is he:* Paul assuredly must have been referring to his mind when he wrote 1Cor. 9:27: *But I keep under my body, and bring it into subjection:*
....and bringing into captivity every thought to the obedience of Christ: The subject to which verse 5 relates is "the mighty weapons of our warfare", verse 4.

6 And having in a readiness to revenge all disobedience, when your obedience is fulfilled.

More clearly to be understood, I believe the verse would be written as, "I am ready to discipline the false teachers and the dissenters among you when you, the faithful among you, completely support me in the disciplinary actions I take."

The Jamieson-Fausset-Brown commentary gives the following on this verse:
"when your obedience, etc. — He charitably assumes that most of the Corinthian Church will act obediently; therefore, he says "YOUR obedience." But perhaps some will act otherwise; in order, therefore, to give all an opportunity of joining the obedient, he will not prematurely exact punishment, but wait until the full number of those gathered out to Christ has been 'completed,' and the remainder have been proved incorrigible."

7 Do ye look on things after the outward appearance? If any man trust to himself that he is Christ's, let him of himself think this again, that, as he is Christ's, even so are we Christ's.

The leader of the dissenters in the Corinthian church was a politician in every sense of the word. He must have possessed great poise, argued convincingly, probably financially affluent, and a forceful leader. Those he regarded as underlings apparently groveled for his praise. He became their voice. None of this made him a child of God, though he hotly contended that he was. Paul wrote, *"If any man trust to himself that he is Christ's...."* He was emphasizing the words, *"trust to himself."* He replied to the claim with the truth, *"we who are Christ's".*

Do ye look on things after the outward appearance? Paul's sarcasm is thinly veiled in this sentence. His question conveys the thought, "What's wrong with your thinking? *For the LORD seeth not as man seeth; for man looketh on the outward appearance, but the LORD looketh on the heart* (I Samuel 16:7). As he had before accused them as being carnal, so accused he again. It is as though he was saying, "Pray more, seek God. Don't allow yourselves to be led astray by ungodly men, no matter how much their physical appearance may appeal to you."

8 For though I should boast somewhat more of our authority, which the Lord hath given us for edification, and not for your destruction, I should not be ashamed:

The Merriam-Webster Collegiate dictionary links boasting to bragging, and bragging to mean "to speak or behave in an arrogant, pompous manner." The word might more properly be understood as "with a feeling of pride; of thankfulness". It probably should be understood as "an assertion, a qualified claim". The latter definition seems to be a more correct translation for "boast" in verse eight.

Jamieson-Fausset-Brown offered this comment:
"For even if I were to boast somewhat more exceedingly (than I do, 2Cor. 10:3-6) of our (apostolic) authority (2Cor.10:6; 2Cor. 13:10) ... I should not be put to shame (by the fact; as I should be if my authority proved to be without foundation: my threats of punishment not being carried into effect)."

9 That I may not seem as if I would terrify you by letters.

Paul assuredly must have written with the same power of persuasion with which he preached. He preached a living, resurrected Christ, who had paid the penalty for sin that all men could be saved. His message was one of impending judgment for all sinners, no matter their race. His ministry was accompanied with signs, wonders, and miracles. The rankest of sinners succumbed to the power of his preaching. His letters must have presented the same terror as that with which he preached.

10 For his letters, say they, are weighty and powerful; but his bodily presence is weak, and his speech contemptible.

...say they: Several commentaries give the thought that it was a ringleader, a dominant person, who led and spoke for the dissenting rebels in the church at Corinth. In whatever way that may be a right interpretation, the two words, say they, tell us that multiple persons in that church were also indicated. That fact might better explain the dissenters' contention that Paul wrote terrifying letters. "*But...his speech is disgusting!*" some claimed. Evidently, losers consistently refuse to give up and admit that they are wrong!

11 Let such an one think this, that, such as we are in word by letters when we are absent, such will we be also in deed when we are present.

Let such an one... The dominant speaker for the rebels in the church is here indicated. Every time I read those few words, I'm immediately struck with the thought, "I wouldn't trade places with that guy for anything!" The verse in paraphrase would read: "Let this loudmouth know that when we come that he will find us just as terrifying in presence as we have been in our letters."

Barnes commented on this verse in the following:
"Let such an one think this ... - Let them not flatter themselves that there will be any discrepancy between my words and my deeds. Let them feel that all which has been threatened will be certainly executed unless there is repentance. Paul here designedly contradicts the charge which was made against him; and means to say that all that he had threatened in his letters would he certainly executed unless there was a reform. I think that the evidence here is clear that Paul does not intend to admit what they said about his bodily presence to be true..."

12 For we dare not make ourselves of the number, or compare ourselves with some that commend themselves: but they measuring themselves by themselves, and comparing themselves among themselves, are not wise.

For we dare not make ourselves of the number: Had Paul and those with him endeavored to appease the rebels, they would have endorsed them by their attempt. There was a war of spirits to be fought once Paul arrived at Corinth, and he, thankfully, refused to settle for an armistice; a clear victory had to be won.

...comparing themselves among themselves, are not wise. How wise can it be for a conglomerate of crooks to cast a ballot to determine which is the worst crook among them? I believe that question delivers the very essence of this verse. If everyone is the same height, why measure to see who is the tallest?

13 But we will not boast of things without our measure, but according to the measure of the rule which God hath distributed to us, a measure to reach even unto you.

Boast should here be understood as "laying claim to" as though the sentence would read, "But we will not lay claim to or take credit for things we haven't accomplished."

...without our measure: Translated as, "beyond our authority" as in "ministered with the authority and power God has given us".

...a measure to reach even unto you: Though Paul spent 18 months in establishing the church at Corinth, many problematic issues still remained to be addressed. He hadn't been able to convince everyone, thus the words, *to reach even unto you.*

14 For we stretch not ourselves beyond our measure, as though we reached not unto you: for we are come as far as to you also in preaching the gospel of Christ:

For we stretch not ourselves beyond our measure: "We haven't exceeded our authority in Christ." The Apostle later wrote in II Cor. 11:6: *But though I be rude in speech, yet not in knowledge; but we have been thoroughly* made manifest *among you in all things.* And again later, in II Cor. 12:12, he wrote: *Truly the signs of an apostle were wrought among you in all patience, in signs, and wonders, and mighty deeds.* All this fell on the deaf ears of the dissenters.

...as though we reached not unto you: The dissenters in the church had not been changed. It was as though Paul and company had not ministered at all to them. Paul refused to accept the blame.

15 Not boasting of things without our measure, that is, of other men's labours; but having hope, when your faith is increased, that we shall be enlarged by you according to our rule abundantly,

Paul was saying that he would take no credit for the success of other ministries that had converted sinners in regions where he had not preached, but... And with that thought in mind, he continued, *...but having hope, when your faith is increased, that we shall be enlarged by you* (rewarded because of your obedience to the faith) *according to our rule abundantly* (as you abundantly willingly obeyed us, enabling us... *"to preach the gospel"* (verse 16).

16 (enabling us) To preach the gospel in the regions beyond you, and not to boast in another man's line of things made ready to our hand.

If Paul's total surrender to Jesus Christ and his eagerness to preach the Gospel where none other had preached it, his zeal for God certainly does shine like a beacon for all to behold.

17 But he that glorieth, let him glory in the Lord.

Jesus said, *"I am the vine, ye are the branches: He that abideth in me, and I in him, the same bringeth forth much fruit: for without me ye can do nothing."* (John 15:5)

Mammoth-size church buildings and vast numbers of congregants don't excite the Lord, but... *The LORD is nigh unto them that are of a broken heart; and saveth such as be of a contrite spirit (*Psalm 34:18).

For all those things hath mine hand made, and all those things have been, saith the LORD: but to this man will I look, even to him that is poor and of a contrite spirit, and trembleth at my word (Isaiah 66:2).

18 For not he that commendeth himself is approved, but whom the Lord commendeth.

Better written, the verse would read: *For he that commendeth himself is not approved, but whom the Lord commendeth* is approved.

For who maketh thee to differ from another? and what hast thou that thou didst not receive? now if thou didst receive it, why dost thou glory, as if thou hadst not received it? (1Cor. 4:7)

Bob Koonce Th. D.

CHAPTER ELEVEN

1 Would to God ye could bear with me a little in my folly: and indeed bear with me.

2 For I am jealous over you with godly jealousy: for I have espoused you to one husband, that I may present you as a chaste virgin to Christ.

3 But I fear, lest by any means, as the serpent beguiled Eve through his subtilty, so your minds should be corrupted from the simplicity that is in Christ.

4 For if he that cometh preacheth another Jesus, whom we have not preached, or if ye receive another spirit, which ye have not received, or another gospel, which ye have not accepted, ye might well bear with him.

5 For I suppose I was not a whit behind the very chiefest apostles.

6 But though I be rude in speech, yet not in knowledge; but we have been throughly made manifest among you in all things.

7 Have I committed an offence in abasing myself that ye might be exalted, because I have preached to you the gospel of God freely?

8 I robbed other churches, taking wages of them, to do you service.

9 And when I was present with you, and wanted, I was chargeable to no man: for that which was lacking to me the brethren which came from Macedonia supplied: and in all things I have kept myself from being burdensome unto you, and so will I keep myself.

10 As the truth of Christ is in me, no man shall stop me of this boasting in the regions of Achaia.

11 Wherefore? because I love you not? God knoweth.

12 But what I do, that I will do, that I may cut off occasion from them which desire occasion; that wherein they glory, they may be found even as we.

13 For such are false apostles, deceitful workers, transforming themselves into the apostles of Christ.

14 And no marvel; for Satan himself is transformed into an angel of light.

15 Therefore it is no great thing if his ministers also be of light.

transformed as the ministers of righteousness; whose end shall be according to their works.

16 I say again, Let no man think me a fool; if otherwise, yet as a fool receive me, that I may boast myself a little.

17 That which I speak, I speak it not after the Lord, but as it were foolishly, in this confidence of boasting.

18 Seeing that many glory after the flesh, I will glory also.

19 For ye suffer fools gladly, seeing ye yourselves are wise.

20 For ye suffer, if a man bring you into bondage, if a man devour you, if a man take of you, if a man exalt himself, if a man smite you on the face.

21 I speak as concerning reproach, as though we had been weak. Howbeit whereinsoever any is bold, (I speak foolishly,) I am bold also.

22 Are they Hebrews? so am I. Are they Israelites? so am I. Are they the seed of Abraham? so am I.

23 Are they ministers of Christ? (I speak as a fool) I am more; in labours more abundant, in stripes above measure, in prisons more frequent, in deaths oft.

24 Of the Jews five times received I forty stripes save one.

25 Thrice was I beaten with rods, once was I stoned, thrice I suffered shipwreck, a night and a day I have been in the deep;

26 In journeyings often, in perils of waters, in perils of robbers, in perils by mine own countrymen, in perils by the heathen, in perils in the city, in perils in the wilderness, in perils in the sea, in perils among false brethren;

27 In weariness and painfulness, in watchings often, in hunger and thirst, in fastings often, in cold and nakedness.

28 Beside those things that are without, that which cometh upon me daily, the care of all the churches.

29 Who is weak, and I am not weak? who is offended, and I burn not?

30 If I must needs glory, I will glory of the things which concern mine infirmities.

31 The God and Father of our Lord Jesus Christ, which is blessed for evermore, knoweth that I lie not.

32 In Damascus the governor under Aretas the king kept the city of the Damascenes with a garrison, desirous to apprehend me:

33 And through a window in a basket was I let down by the wall, and escaped his hands.

Seeming weariness in Paul at times is detected, and that vividly demonstrates that though he proved himself as a powerful persuader, still as a human, he was bound to all the limitations of humanity. He experienced "a thorn in the flesh," of which we know little, yet he persevered. Having to repeatedly indoctrinate former heathens to Christianity taxed him, but dissenters among his converts deeply troubled him. All this is discussed in this chapter. Perhaps the reader will also detect a weariness in Paul.

1Would to God ye could bear with me a little in my folly: and indeed bear with me.

The Merriam-Webster Collegiate Dictionary gives 5 definitions for folly. I think 2 definitions apply to the word as it is used in this verse:
Lack of good sense or normal prudence.
A foolish act or idea.
Strong's number 878 gives 3 definitions
Senselessness
Egotism
Restlessness

According to the dissenters in the church at Corinth, all 5 definitions applied to Paul. That wise apostle was well aware of their accusations. When he wrote, "Bear with me," he was not pleading for their patience. Rather, he was demanding that they keep silent and listen patiently when his letter was being read aloud to the congregation. *Bear with me…indeed.* Hush! Paul had written much, and he dared hope that the letter would produce positive results.

Clarke's Commentary gave the following opinion on this verse: In my folly - In my seeming folly; for, being obliged to vindicate his ministry, it was necessary that he should speak much of himself, his sufferings, and his success. And as this would appear like boasting; and boasting is always the effect of an empty, foolish mind; those who were not acquainted with the necessity that lay upon him to make this defense, might be led to impute it to vanity. As if he had said: Suppose you allow this to be folly, have the good-

-ness to bear with me; for though I glory, I should not be a fool, 2Cor. 12:6. And let no man think me a fool for my boasting, 2Cor. 11:16."

2 For I am jealous over you with godly jealousy: for I have espoused you to one husband, that I may present you as a chaste virgin to Christ.

Jealous: Merriam-Webster gives 1 definition for jealousy that describes Paul well: "Vigilant in guarding a possession." How better could Paul's care for the churches of God be described? As a father guiding his children through extreme dangers, so did Paul attempt to guide faithful Christians.

I have espoused you to one husband: Strong's' Concordance number 719 defines *"espouse"* as "to joint".

Easton's 1897 Bible Dictionary defines "espouse" as: To betroth. The espousal was a ceremony of betrothing, a formal agreement between the parties then coming under obligation for the purpose of marriage. Espousals are in the East frequently contracted years before the marriage is celebrated. It is referred to as figuratively illustrating the relations between God and his people (Jer. 2:2; Matt. 1:18; 2 Cor. 11:2).

An espousal or betrothal ceremony was binding on the involved couple. It was a period of preparation for the coming marriage ceremony. Its purpose was to initiate a dedication in the one to the other, between the bride and the groom. It did not allow physical union between the two until after the marriage ceremony was observed. And it is in this fact that the doctrine of Eternal Security is faulted.

Eternal Security assures its followers that once saved, always saved. From the statement that once saved always saved, it must be understood in the same sense as "once engaged to marry is to be always engaged to marry." That conception is erroneous. Repentance for sins is not salvation completed, else people would be saved over and over, for Christians need to repent for intentional and unintentional sins they commit during their life spans. Paul's words, *I have espoused you to one husband,* informs a Christian that there is no room for "extra husbands-extra love affairs with sin" in their life.

...that I may present you as a chaste virgin to Christ. "Pure in thought and act" (Merriam-Webster) and verified by the Word of God. How powerfully this does condemn stubbornness, sin, and rebellion! As a chaste virgin—2 words that deliver the same message. How hard must Paul's soul have been vexed as he coaxed the Corinthians from fault after fault in his undying effort to present them as pure and unspoiled to Christ!

3 But I fear, lest by any means, as the serpent beguiled Eve through his subtilty, so your minds should be corrupted from the simplicity that is in Christ.

Eve was taken from Adam, who was perfectly formed, thus she must also have been perfect in form. She must have been rather intelligent as opposed to the rather common concept that her intelligence may have been equal to no more than that of a child. That she was deceived does not mean that she was simple-minded. In fact, it proves the opposite. She knew the consequence for eating the forbidden fruit, but in her innocence, she did not realize that the beautiful creature that faced and persuaded her was pure evil. There is no information preserved to inform us how long the devil persuaded her. It may have taken hours, days, months, even years for her to capitulate, but then she looked at the fruit and saw it was good to eat. Deceit had been completed.

Satan did not assault Eve in any manner; he worked on her mind. It is said that Hitler claimed that if a lie is told long enough and often enough, that people would eventually believe it to be truth. That's the very tactic that Satan used on Eve, and the very tactic that Paul feared the devil would use on his beloved Corinthian believers. "*Lest by any means,*" he wrote, "*as the serpent beguiled Eve.*"

Jamieson-Faucett-Brown Commentary supplies the following on verse 3.
"subtilty — the utter foe of the "simplicity" which is intent on ONE object, Jesus, and seeks none 'other,' and no 'other' and

different Spirit (2Cor.11:4); but loves him with tender SINGLENESS OF AFFECTION. Where Eve first gave way, was in mentally harboring for a moment the possibility insinuated by the serpent, of God not having her truest interests at heart, and of this 'other' professing friend being more concerned for her than God."

4 For if he that cometh preacheth another Jesus, whom we have not preached, or if ye receive another spirit, which ye have not received, or another gospel, which ye have not accepted, ye might well bear with him.

Without doubt, it would seem, Paul addressed the dissenters and rebels in the Corinthian church. Yet, previously, he scolded all of them for allowing themselves to place admiration for a man ahead of their love for God and his servants. In identifying the type of men they might well receive, Paul here alluded to Jude 1:16: *These are murmurers, complainers, walking after their own lusts; and their mouth speaketh great swelling words, having men's persons in admiration because of advantage.* Paraphrased, this verse would read: "They will bowl you over with their praises for you, and you will let them deceive you." Galatians 1:8 declares: *But though we, or an angel from heaven, preach any other gospel unto you than that which we have preached unto you, let him be accursed*

5 For I suppose I was not a whit behind the very chiefest apostles.

This verse conveys an important message about humility. In essence, Paul said, "You want someone who is very important, someone highly acclaimed. Well, you apparently have ignored the fact that the most important apostles were no greater than I am! We're on the same level. Yet, I have abased myself to serve you at no cost to you whatsoever. Still you accept someone you don't know and reject those who have proven themselves to you."

6 But though I be rude in speech, yet not in knowledge; but we have been throughly made manifest among you in all things.

The word, rude, is nowhere else used in the New Testament. Bible commentators accept this intentional slur on Paul as being fact. I think that concept to probably be wrong.

But though I be rude in speech... May we not miss the word, though, in this verse. The verse could well be worded, "You say that I speak rudely, but that is an intentional slur. But even if that were true, which it is not, yet there is no way you can degrade my knowledge."

...we have been throughly made manifest among you in all things. Oh, how Paul's detractors must have hated that fact! Manifest: "Easily understood or recognized by the mind." (Merriam-Webster). Paul attacked their evil minds further by writing, *made manifest* (made known) *among you in all things.*

Throughly: As used in this verse, I think this word perhaps should be left undisturbed. It is translated into modern English as, thoroughly. Throughly is defined as "in a thorough manner". I think there is a subtle difference. While Paul was thorough in his teaching and training, yet he had to go through their minds to correct their souls, thus, *"we have been throughly made manifest among you in all things."*

7 Have I committed an offence in abasing, because I have preached to you the gospel of God freely?

This verse would better read if it were rearranged: *Because I have abused myself and preached to you the gospel of God freely, have I committed an offence?* Thieves experience no shame in stealing from others to satisfy their own lusts. It is that same spirit the rebels in the Corinthian church used in their attempt to soil Paul's character.

Unlike many other commentaries, the Geneva renders the following comment:

"Another slander, that is, that he was a rascal, and lived by the labour of his own hands. But in this, the apostle says, what can you lay against me, except that I was content to take any pains for your sakes? For when I lacked, I travailed for my living with my own hands. And also, when poverty forced me, I chose rather to seek my sustenance than to be any burden to you, even though I preached the Gospel to you."

For better clarity, I have taken the liberty of chronologically rearranging a few verses.

9 And when I was present with you, and wanted, I was chargeable to no man: for that which was lacking to me the brethren which came from Macedonia supplied: and in all things I have kept myself from being burdensome unto you, and so will I keep myself.

Paul mentioned several times that the Corinthian church supported him with supplies intermittently, and at times, not at all. This seems so unclear as it relates to a church where Paul ministered for 18 months. It, however, highly commends Paul for his unselfish character and willingness to sacrifice his own life, if necessary, to further the Gospel of Jesus Christ.

"The brethren which came from Macedonia - He probably refers to the supplies which he received from the Church at Philippi, which was in Macedonia; of which he says, that in the beginning of the Gospel no Church communicated with me, as concerning giving and receiving, but you (Philippi) only; for even at Thessalonica ye sent once and again to my necessity." (Clarke)

10 As the truth of Christ is in me, no man shall stop me of this boasting in the regions of Achaia.

"Boasting" should here be understood as "laying claim to; as asserting." He was not bragging. Paul had enjoyed much success at Corinth despite the lingering problems there at the time of his writing. When he spoke of "boast" he referred to the power of God demonstrated by the conversions of numerous heathen worshippers to Jesus Christ.

11 Wherefore? because I love you not? God knoweth.

Wherefore? I am a little more than simply puzzled that several commentators understand this as saying, "Why do I not accept help from you?" The word, wherefore, connects directly with the "boasting" in the preceding verse. Their question was: "Why do you tell other churches about our lack of support for you? Do you no longer love us?" Paul replied, "God knows the reason." Their quest-

-ion was for the purpose of putting him on the defensive. While we might wish he had explained the reason in detail, he knew that they knew the reason and no more needed to be written on the subject.

8 I robbed other churches, taking wages of them, to do you service.

I view the message that this verse delivers, is as though Paul wrote: I took help from other churches because I was hungry. I was in your service. You neglected to supply my basic needs. Other churches saw and took your place; you were robbed of a blessing you should not have yielded. Shame! I could have insisted that you feed me, but that would have made me your hireling and not your servant.

Barnes' notes give more on this verse:
"I robbed other churches - The churches of Macedonia and elsewhere, which had ministered to his needs. Probably he refers especially to the church at Philippi (see Philippians 4:15-16), which seems to have done more than almost any other church for his support. By the use of the word "robbed" here Paul does not mean that he had obtained anything from them in a violent or unlawful manner, or anything which they did not give voluntarily."

12 But what I do, that I will do, that I may cut off occasion from them which desire occasion; that wherein they glory, they may be found even as we.

But what I do, that I will do. "I have said all that I need to say to the rebels. I will not present another *occasion* (opportunity) for the trouble-making, false prophets there to pounce onto something else I have written in order to make themselves to appear as apostles also."

13 For such are false apostles, deceitful workers, transforming themselves into the apostles of Christ.
14 And no marvel; for Satan himself is transformed into an angel of light.
15 Therefore it is no great thing if his ministers also be transformed as the ministers of righteousness; whose end shall be according to their works.

The devil refuses to accept the guilt for his fall from God's presence. The name, Lucifer, speaks of light. A common wood match is also known as a lucifer and extinguishes shortly after being lighted. The devil's light has gone out forever. He cannot be seen by the eye, but he appears in many disguises. It seems that his favorite disguise is in the form of greedy preachers, false teachers, and false prophets intent on persuading those ready to be beguiled to become their followers.

16 I say again, Let no man think me a fool; if otherwise, yet as a fool receive me, that I may boast myself a little.

Fool: The word is translated from the Greek word, *aphon*, and properly can be understood as ignorant, stupid, and mindless. Now notice the incongruity of their effort to defame Paul. The very people that dared call Paul stupid must have listened to his teaching many times during the 18 months of his ministry in Corinth. The rebels would not have dared call him ignorant while he was there with them. But their cowardice and rebellion came into full bloom after he was gone. Paul called their bluff when, in essence, he said, "You listened to me while I was there with you, and you didn't object then to my teaching. I haven't changed. If I am a fool now, I was a fool when you listened to me then so, apparently, we are fellow-fools!"

...yet as a fool receive me: "If I were indeed a fool as you called me, I am going to boast as a fool would boast—as you would boast."

17 That which I speak, I speak it not after the Lord, but as it were foolishly, in this confidence of boasting.

I speak it not after the Lord: "That which I will speak as a fool would boast, will not be as the Lord would have me speak. I'm going to brag like a fool would brag, so listen."

18 Seeing that many glory after the flesh, I will glory also.

...after the flesh: As a human without God would boast. Barnes' Commentary adds further thoughts on this verse:
"Seeing that many glory ... - The false teachers in Corinth. They

boasted of their birth, rank, natural endowments, eloquence, etc.;

I will glory also - I also will boast of my endowments, which though somewhat different yet pertain in the main to the "flesh". His endowments "in the flesh," or what he had to boast of pertaining to the flesh, related not so much to birth and rank, though not inferior to them in these, but to what the flesh had endured - to stripes and imprisonments, and hunger and peril. This is an exceedingly delicate and happy turn given to the whole subject."

19 For ye suffer fools gladly, seeing ye yourselves are wise.

I think Paul's intended message of this verse would read: You brag that you are wise, but as fools (stupid, ignorant, mindless men) you fellowship fools (mindless, ignorant, stupid), men like you.

"This is perhaps the most sarcastic sentence ever penned by the apostle Paul" (Dr. Bloomfield)

20 For ye suffer, if a man bring you into bondage, if a man devour you, if a man take of you, if a man exalt himself, if a man smite you on the face.

"For ye suffer" - As you are so meek and gentle as to submit to be brought into bondage, to have your property devoured, your goods taken away, yourselves laid in the dust, so that others may exalt themselves over you, yea, and will bear from those the most degrading indignity; then of course, you will bear with one who has never insulted, defrauded, devoured, taken of you, exalted himself against you, or offered you any kind of indignity; and who only wishes you to bear his confident boasting, concerning matters which he can substantiate.

"The expressions in this verse are some evidence that the false apostle was a Judaizing teacher. You suffer, says the apostle, if a man, καταδουλοι, bring you into bondage, probably meaning to the Jewish rites and ceremonies, Gal. 4:9; Gal. 5:1. If he devour you; as the Pharisees did the patrimony of the widows, and for a pretense made long prayers; if a man take of you, exact different contributions, pretendedly for the temple at Jerusalem, etc. If he exalt himself, pretending to be of the seed of Abraham, infinitely higher in honor and dignity than all the families of the Gentiles; if he smite you on the face - treat you with indignity, as the Jews did the Gentiles, considering them only as dogs, and not fit to be ranked with any of the descendants of Jacob." (Clarke)

21 I speak as concerning reproach, as though we had been weak. Howbeit whereinsoever any is bold, (I speak foolishly,) I am bold also.

I speak as concerning reproach: It remains a mystery why generosity is often despised and defamed while oppression is first approached with curiosity then meekly accepted.

Paul asked, "Why do you think of us as being weak? You desire boldness; I am bold in verifying my qualifications as an apostle."

In verse 23, Paul stated that, *I speak as a fool*, meaning he spoke as an unregenerate man would boast.

In verses 22-29, he substantiates his qualifications for his apostleship.

22 Are they Hebrews? so am I. Are they Israelites? so am I. Are they the seed of Abraham? so am I.
23 Are they ministers of Christ? (I speak as a fool) I am more; in labours more abundant, in stripes above measure, in prisons more frequent, in deaths oft.
24 Of the Jews five times received I forty stripes save one.

"Of the Jews five times received I forty stripes save one - That is, he was five times scourged by the Jews, whose law (Deut. 25:3) allowed forty stripes; but they, pretending to be lenient, and to act within the letter of the law, inflicted but thirty-nine. To except one stripe from the forty was a very ancient canon among the Jews." (Clarke)

25 Thrice was I beaten with rods, once was I stoned, thrice I suf-

-fered shipwreck, a night and a day I have been in the deep;

"Thrice was I beaten with rods - This was under the Roman government, as their lictors beat criminals in this way. We hear of the apostle's being treated thus once, namely at Philippi, Acts 16:22.

"Once was I stoned - Namely, at Lystra, Acta 14:19.

"A night and a day I have been in the deep - To what this refers we cannot tell; it is generally supposed that in some shipwreck not on record the apostle had saved himself on a plank, and was a whole day and night on the sea, tossed about at the mercy of the waves." (Clarke)

26 In journeyings often, in perils of waters, in perils of robbers, in perils by mine own countrymen, in perils by the heathen, in perils in the city, in perils in the wilderness, in perils in the sea, in perils among false brethren;

"*...in perils of waters*: The waters mentioned here must refer to waters in rivers, creeks, etc. He mentioned *perils in the sea* later in this verse, so he evidently meant waters other that the sea.

"Of robbers - Judea itself, and perhaps every other country, was grievously infested by banditti of this kind; and no doubt the apostle in his frequent peregrinations was often attacked, but, being poor and having nothing to lose, he passed unhurt, though not without great danger.

"In perils by mine own countrymen - The Jews had the most rooted antipathy to him, because they considered him an apostate from the true faith, and also the means of perverting many others. There are several instances of this in the Acts; and a remarkable conspiracy against his life is related, Acts 23:12, etc.

"In perils by the heathen - In the heathen provinces whither he went to preach the Gospel. Several instances of these perils occur also in the Acts.

"In perils in the city - The different seditions raised against him; particularly in Jerusalem, to which Ephesus and Damascus may be added.

"Perils in the wilderness - Uninhabited countries through which he was obliged to pass in order to reach from city to city. In such places it is easy to imagine many dangers from banditti, wild beasts, cold, starvation, etc.

"Perils in the sea - The different voyages he took in narrow seas, such as the Mediterranean, about dangerous coasts, and without compass.

"False brethren - Persons who joined themselves to the Church, pretending faith in Christ, but intending to act as spies, hoping to get some matter of accusation against him. He no doubt suffered much also from apostates." (Clarke)

27 In weariness and painfulness, in watchings often, in hunger and thirst, in fastings often, in cold and nakedness.

"In weariness and painfulness - Tribulations of this kind were his constant companions. Lord Lyttleton and others have made useful reflections on this verse: 'How hard was it for a man of a genteel and liberal education, as St. Paul was, to bear such rigors, and to wander about like a vagabond, hungry and almost naked, yet coming into the presence of persons of high life, and speaking in large and various assemblies on matters of the utmost importance!' Had not St. Paul been deeply convinced of the truth and absolute certainty of the Christian religion, he could not have continued to expose himself to such hardships." (Clarke)

28 Beside those things that are without, that which cometh upon me daily, the care of all the churches.

...the care of all the churches: Jesus said, *I am the good shepherd: the good shepherd giveth his life for the sheep* (John 10:11). And such was Paul's burden and care for the churches he founded. Without modern forms of communication, news concerning certain churches had to come by courier. Paul naturally was anxious during those times of waiting. And while news was long in coming, the Apostle fasted, prayed, and preached during intervals. He wrote letters. He was never silent about the Gospel of Jesus Christ.

29 Who is weak, and I am not weak? who is offended, and I burn not?

...who is offended, and I burn not? Did Paul get angry? Certainly! Paul was human. I suppose it impossible to imagine the depth of the hurt he felt when converts turned from him to false teachers and joined in the abuse of him and to false charges made against him.

30 If I must needs glory, I will glory of the things which concern mine infirmities.

If I must needs glory: "You compel me to boast as you would boast in order to verify the legitimacy of my ministry. You demand evidence—I give you the best confirmation available. Read on."

31 The God and Father of our Lord Jesus Christ, which is blessed for evermore, knoweth that I lie not.

"This solemn asseveration refers to what follows. The persecution at Damascus was one of the first and greatest and having no human witness of it to adduce to the Corinthians, as being a fact that happened long before and was known to few, he appeals to God for its truth. Luke (Acts 9:25) afterwards recorded it (compare Gal. 1:20), [Bengel]. It may ALSO refer to the revelation in 2Cor. 12:1, standing in beautiful contrast to his humiliating escape from Damascus." (Jamieson-Fausset-Brown)

32 In Damascus the governor under Aretas the king kept the city of the Damascenes with a garrison, desirous to apprehend me:

governor — *Greek,* "Ethnarch": a Jewish officer to whom heathen rulers gave authority over Jews in large cities where they were numerous. He was in this case under Aretas, king of Arabia. (Jamieson-Faucett-Brown)

33 And through a window in a basket was I let down by the wall, and escaped his hands.

The former persecutor of Christians became the intended quarry of the Jews that once viewed him as a valuable asset. The Jews in the city were so politically powerful as to cause the Roman authorities to employ an entire garrison to prevent the Apostle's escape from the city. How powerful the young man, Paul, had become so early in his Christian experience!

CHAPTER TWELVE

1 It is not expedient for me doubtless to glory. I will come to visions and revelations of the Lord.

2 I knew a man in Christ above fourteen years ago, (whether in the body, I cannot tell; or whether out of the body, I cannot tell: God knoweth;) such an one caught up to the third heaven.

3 And I knew such a man, (whether in the body, or out of the body, I cannot tell: God knoweth;)

4 How that he was caught up into paradise, and heard unspeakable words, which it is not lawful for a man to utter.

5 Of such an one will I glory: yet of myself I will not glory, but in mine infirmities.

6 For though I would desire to glory, I shall not be a fool; for I will say the truth: but now I forbear, lest any man should think of me above that which he seeth me to be, or that he heareth of me.

7 And lest I should be exalted above measure through the abundance of the revelations, there was given to me a thorn in the flesh, the messenger of Satan to buffet me, lest I should be exalted above measure.

8 For this thing I besought the Lord thrice, that it might depart from me.

9 And he said unto me, My grace is sufficient for thee: for my strength is made perfect in weakness. Most gladly therefore will I rather glory in my infirmities, that the power of Christ may rest upon me.

10 Therefore I take pleasure in infirmities, in reproaches, in necessities, in persecutions, in distresses for Christ's sake: for when I am weak, then am I strong.

11 I am become a fool in glorying; ye have compelled me: for I ought to have been commended of you: for in nothing am I behind the very chiefest apostles, though I be nothing.

12 Truly the signs of an apostle were wrought among you in all patience, in signs, and wonders, and mighty deeds.

13 For what is it wherein ye were inferior to other churches, except it be that I myself was not burdensome to you? forgive me this wrong.

14 Behold, the third time I am ready to come to you; and I will not be burdensome to you: for I seek not yours, but you: for the children ought not to lay up for the parents, but the parents for the children.

15 And I will very gladly spend and be spent for you; though the more abundantly I love you, the less I be loved.

16 But be it so, I did not burden you: nevertheless, being crafty, I caught you with guile.

17 Did I make a gain of you by any of them whom I sent unto you?

18 I desired Titus, and with him I sent a brother. Did Titus make a gain of you? walked we not in the same spirit? walked we not in the same steps?

19 Again, think ye that we excuse ourselves unto you? we speak before God in Christ: but we do all things, dearly beloved, for your edifying.

20 For I fear, lest, when I come, I shall not find you such as I would, and that I shall be found unto you such as ye would not: lest there be debates, envyings, wraths, strifes, backbitings, whisperings, swellings, tumults:

21And lest, when I come again, my God will humble me among you, and that I shall bewail many which have sinned already, and have not repented of the uncleanness and fornication and lasciviousness which they have committed.

This chapter does not introduce a new subject. Its first verse continues Paul's effort to wrest false doctrines and false assumptions from the minds of some in the Corinthian church who had been deceived by ungodly teachers. In consulting several commentaries that address the first verse, I naturally found many opinions. It is not strange that nearly all teachers sometime interpret as they understand the environment, the atmosphere of the period of time in which they live. But may we understand Paul's writings in the atmosphere in which they were written. Personally, I find this difficult and challenging, but the words of chapter 13:1--*In the mouth of two or three witnesses shall every word be established*—provides a guideline I endeavor to follow. Now for verse 1:

1 It is not expedient for me doubtless to glory. I will come to visions and revelations of the Lord.

...not expedient for me doubtless to glory: Expedient is a word meaning, "suitable for achieving a particular goal in a given situation". Paul did not need to glory, or brag, as the meaning is here intended for the word. With or without the Corinthians, Paul stood a giant among all others. He was very aware of that fact and had only mentioned it in chapter 12 for the specific purpose to contradict the false apostles among the Corinthians.

Some commentators are of the opinion that instead of the wording to be "not expedient", rather to be, "it is expedient." They expressed that they believed that Paul felt compelled to mention his qualifications for his apostleship to counter the claims of the false apostles within the church. Both opinions bear merit. I am inclined to believe that the KJV version is correct as written. However, I here insert an excerpt from Gill on the phrase:

"Some copies, and the Vulgate Latin version, read, "if there was need of glorying, it is not indeed expedient"; the Syriac version, "there is need of glorying, but it is not expedient"; and the Arabic version, "neither have I need to glory, nor is it expedient for me: I will come to visions and revelations of the Lord";

I agree with the Arabic version. I think that Paul's next words in this verse--*I will come to visions*—translate: "I proceed now to the subject of visions."

2 I knew a man in Christ above fourteen years ago, (whether in the body, I cannot tell; or whether out of the body, I cannot tell: God knoweth;) such an one caught up to the third heaven.

I believe that Paul here spoke of his stoning and being left for dead at Lystra. The time in which he penned this verse coincides with his stoning 14 years prior. He wrote: *such an one caught up to the third heaven.*

Barnes' Commentary comments thus on this expression:
"To the third heaven - The Jews sometimes speak of seven heavens, and Muhammed has borrowed this idea from the Jews. But the Bible speaks of but three heavens, and among the Jews in

the apostolic ages also the heavens were divided into three:

"(1) The aerial, including the clouds and the atmosphere, the heavens above us, until we come to the stars.
(2) The starry heavens, the heavens in which the sun, moon, and stars appear to be situated.
(3) The heavens beyond the stars. That heaven was supposed to be the residence of God, of angels, and of holy spirits. It was this upper heaven, the dwelling-place of God, to which Paul was taken, and whose wonders he was permitted to behold"

Paul declined to say that the stoning killed him, but the stoners, and even his companions, were convinced that he was dead.

3 And I knew such a man, (whether in the body, or out of the body, I cannot tell: God knoweth;)

The Jamieson-Fausset-Brown Commentary translates "knew" as "know". Either word affirms a personal knowledge of the man—namely himself. His humility was always in evidence. Though he had used the language, *"for in nothing am I behind the very chiefest apostles"* in 12:11, he still regarded himself as Ephesians 3:8 declares: "*Unto me, who am less than the least of all saints, is this grace given, that I should preach among the Gentiles the unsearchable riches of Christ;*"

And I knew (know) *such a man*—personal, intimate knowledge of the person in reference—himself.

4 How that he was caught up into paradise, and heard unspeakable words, which it is not lawful for a man to utter.

...was caught up into paradise: The third heaven is here identified as paradise.

5 Of such an one will I glory: yet of myself I will not glory, but in mine infirmities.

Of such an one will I glory: Modestly speaking of himself so as to receive no accolades for himself personally, he wrote as though addressing another person. The words, *of such an one*, might be more clearly understood as: *of the experience of such an one*. In that *experience* where he saw the glories of paradise and heard words that he was entrusted to not repeat; in that experience, he felt glory, a glory that he couldn't express in mere words.

I will not glory, but in mine infirmities. "I will glory only in my infirmities." Verse 9 of this chapter could well be attached to this phrase. *⁹And he said unto me, My grace is sufficient for thee: for my strength is made perfect in weakness. Most gladly therefore will I rather glory in my infirmities, that the power of Christ may rest upon me.*

The word, "glory", as used in these verses, is sufficiently difficult to define. In the previous chapter, the word, boast, is used as "taking credit for something and assuming authority to repeat it." "Glory" in this chapter carries the connotation of "being blessed; being spiritually uplifted; being strengthened spiritually". So, Paul wrote, "I will glory in my infirmities."

6 For, I shall not be a fool; for I will say the truth: but now I forbear, lest any man should think of me above that which he seeth me to be, or that he heareth of me.

I shall not be a fool, though I would desire to glory reads with the verse reversed. ... *but now I forbear,* he continued, signifying he used strength to quell any fleshly desire to boast. Carnal men boast of things they cannot or did not attain, but Paul wrote, *for I will say the truth.* He continued with the reasoning that if he spoke of the things he rightly and truly had attained, people might actually give him more credit than that due him-- *lest any man should think of me above that which he seeth me to be, or that he heareth of me.*

7 And lest I should be exalted above measure through the abundance of the revelations, there was given to me a thorn in the flesh, the messenger of Satan to buffet me, lest I should be exalted above measure.

...be exalted above measure: I understand this phrase as, "Think of myself more highly than the measure of my faith could contain

me, and I would become proud." Romans 12:3 agrees with that application: *For I say, through the grace given unto me, to every man that is among you, not to think of himself more highly than he ought to think; but to think soberly, according as God hath dealt to every man the measure of faith.*

"…through the abundance of the revelations; for he had not only one or two, or a few, but an abundance of them; and which, as everything does but grace, tended to lift up his mind, to stir up the pride of his heart, and to entertain too high and exalted thoughts of himself. Pride is naturally in every man's heart; converted persons are not without it; knowledge, gifts, and revelations are apt to puff up with spiritual pride, unless counterbalanced and over poised by the grace of God. This great apostle was not out of danger by them, for he was not already perfect; wherefore to prevent an excess of pride and vanity in him on account of them, he says, he was given a thorn in the flesh." (Gill)

"What this thorn in the flesh might be has given birth to a multitude of conjectures: Tertullian thought it *dolor auriculae*, the earache; Chrysostom, κεφαλαλγια, the headache; Cyprian, *carnis et corporis multa ac gravia tormenta*, many and grievous bodily torments." (Clarke)

I have no idea what the thorn in the flesh may have been. Many guess, some debate, but no one can offer definite proof for his/her contention.

8 For this thing I besought the Lord thrice, that it might depart from me.

The thorn seems to have caused great discomfort. Paul besought the Lord three times *"that it might depart from me."* It may have been a mental vexation, a physical pain, a disease in his eyes or body—we are left to guess. Whatever it was, it was a vexation to Paul. He earnestly pleaded that it be removed.

9 And he said unto me, My grace is sufficient for thee: for my strength is made perfect in weakness. Most gladly therefore will I rather glory in my infirmities, that the power of Christ may rest upon me.

So-called faith healers and prosperity preachers pressure their damnable philosophies into the minds and hearts of scripturally ignorant, gullible people. If a person is poor or sick in any way, say they, that person is defying the power of God. Of course, a generous offering to the ministry guarantees that their name will be placed first on their prayer list! Thousands of the gullible respond daily to the charlatans, not knowing that their letters are trashed immediately after their offering has been removed.

My grace is sufficient for thee: for my strength is made perfect in weakness. Paul's thorn was not removed because God knew that he needed it. Had he never had a vexation he could not remove; he could never have felt despair in its constant torment. When exultation approached him, pain tempered its power to overwhelm him. Never was there a time when he did not experience his constant need of God.

10 Therefore I take pleasure in infirmities, in reproaches, in necessities, in persecutions, in distresses for Christ's sake: for when I am weak, then am I strong.

Therefore I take pleasure in infirmities: In Romans 8:28, Paul gave advice he had gained through experience: *And we know that all things work together for good to them that love God, to them who are the called according to his purpose.* He knew that God had called him and set him aside for a particular ministry. Before writing verse 10, Paul had suffered many hardships, torture, and pain. In his being afflicted with a thorn in the flesh that could not be moved, he forced himself to remember that "all things work together for good to them that believe."

11 I am become a fool in glorying; ye have compelled me: for I ought to have been commended of you: for in nothing am I behind the very chiefest apostles, though I be nothing.

I am become a fool in glorying: The words, I am (present tense), should be rendered, I was (past tense). The second clause, "*ye have* (past tense) *compelled me.* Verse 11 refers directly to chapter 11, verses 16-18.

12 Truly the signs of an apostle were wrought among you in all patience, in signs, and wonders, and mighty deeds.

Paul's patience appears slightly threadbare as he continued reasoning with the reluctant Corinthians. The verse seems to convey the message: "What more do you need to convince you? You have witnessed great signs, wonders, and mighty deeds. With what power have the false apostles among you been able to deceive you?"

"The signs of an apostle were wrought among you - Though I have been reputed as nothing, I have given the fullest proof of my Divine mission by various signs, wonders, and miracles, and by that patience which I have manifested towards you: though I had power from God to inflict punishment on the transgressors, I have in every case forborne to do it. Is the man nothing who wrought such miracles among you?" (Clarke)

13 For what is it wherein ye were inferior to other churches, except it be that I myself was not burdensome to you? forgive me this wrong.

Clarke's Commentary gives this application for this veer:
"For what is it wherein you were inferior - This is a fine, forcible, yet delicate stroke. It was your duty and your interest to have supported your apostle; other Churches have done so: I did not require this from you; in this respect, all other Churches are superior to you. I am the cause of your inferiority, by not giving you an opportunity of ministering to my necessities: forgive me the wrong I have done you. It is the privilege of the Churches of Christ to support the ministry of his Gospel among them. Those who do not contribute their part to the support of the Gospel ministry either care nothing for it, or derive no good from it."

14 Behold, the third time I am ready to come to you; and I will not be burdensome to you: for I seek not yours, but you: for the children ought not to lay up for the parents, but the parents for the children.

...third time I am ready to come to you: 2 visits had already been made or 2 epistles had been sent to them. Clarke's and Barnes' commentaries both disagree with that interpretation. Both interpret the verse as saying, "This is the third time *I am ready to come.*" Respectfully, I think that is too easy an interpretation. I question, if he had been ready 2 times previous to this writing, why had he not gone? The Jamieson-Faucett-Brown Commentary agrees with my opinion:

"...the third time —His *second* visit was probably a short one (1Cor. 16:7) and attended with humiliation through the scandalous conduct of some of his converts (compare 2Cor. 12:21; 2Cor. 2:1). It was probably paid during his three years' sojourn at Ephesus, from which he could pass so readily by sea to Corinth (compare 2Cor. 1:15, 2Cor. 1:16; 2Cor. 13:1, 2Cor. 13:2). The context here implies nothing of a *third preparation* to come; but, [as Alford stated] 'I am coming, and the third time, and will not burden you this time any more than I did at my *two previous visits.*" (JFB)

15 And I will very gladly spend and be spent for you; though the more abundantly I love you, the less I be loved.

I will very gladly spend and be spent for you: The first declaration in this verse displays Paul's total unselfishness, his total commitment to Jesus Christ, and his total love for the souls of the Corinthians. Though they had left him hungry and neglected on previous visits, he was anxious to be so used again by them.

...though the more abundantly I love you, the less I be loved. How vividly this statement mirrors John 1:10, *11: He was in the world, and the world was made by him, and the world knew him not.*
11 He came unto his own, and his own received him not.

The Jamieson-Fausset-Brown Commentary gives a concise summation of this verse:
"I will ... spend — all I have.
"be spent — all that I am." This is more than even natural parents do. They "lay up *treasures* for their children."

But I spend not merely my treasures, but *myself.*

"for you — *Greek,* "for your souls"; not for your mere bodies."

"the less I be loved — Love rather descends than ascends [Bengel]. Love him as a true friend who seeks your good more than your good will."

Gill's interpretation renders a more expansive comment on the same verse:

"And I will gladly spend.... Meaning all his time, talents, and strength, which God had bestowed upon him for their spiritual profit and advantage; yea, all that small pittance of worldly goods that he enjoyed: he not only determined to take nothing from them, but was willing to communicate his little substance to them, or spend it in their service; and not only so, but be spent for them:

"and be spent for you, or "for your souls": for the good of them; his sense is, either that he was willing to have his whole substance expended, if it would be of any use to them; or his whole strength exhausted, in laborious preaching to them; or even his life to be laid down for them, was it necessary; which sense is favoured by the Syriac and Arabic versions; all which expressed his tender affection as a spiritual father for them: adding,

"though the more abundantly I love you, the less I be loved; though he loved them more than he did other churches, or than the false apostles loved them, and yet were loved by them less than he was by other churches; or by them, than the false apostles were; or rather the meaning is, that though he increased in his love, and in the expressions of it to them, and they grew colder and more indifferent to him, yet this should not hinder his warmest desires and most earnest endeavours after their spiritual and eternal welfare. This way of speaking strongly expresses his love to them, and tacitly implies the lukewarmness of theirs to him; and yet that it should be no discouragement to him to proceed in doing them all the service he was capable of."

16 But be it so, I did not burden you: nevertheless, being crafty, I caught you with guile.

Rearranged for better understanding, the verse would read: *I, being guilefully crafty, caught you even though I took nothing from you.* The word "crafty" should be replaced with "skillfully", for that is the true sense of the word. Paul was not a crafty schemer intent on deceiving his listeners—the exact opposite of the completely unselfish man that he was.

17 Did I make a gain of you by any of them whom I sent unto you?
18 I desired Titus, and with him I sent a brother. Did Titus make a gain of you? walked we not in the same spirit? walked we not in the same steps?

Verses 17 and 18 deliver the same question: Did Paul, those with him, or any that he sent unto them gain any material wealth from them? The false apostles in the Corinthian had enjoyed much success in poisoning the minds of several in that congregation and rendered them skeptical of Paul.

19 Again, think ye that we excuse ourselves unto you? we speak before God in Christ: but we do all things, dearly beloved, for your edifying.

Again: How wearisome for the Apostle to continue repeating himself, but the contest for the minds and souls of the gullible among the Corinthians was at stake. The verse delivers the sense: "Do you think that we're defending ourselves with excuses? Pay attention to what I say—we speak boldly in Christ in the presence of God! But for you who are so greatly loved, please understand that we do everything for your enrichment, your edification."

20 For I fear, lest, when I come, I shall not find you such as I would, and that I shall be found unto you such as ye would not: lest there be debates, envyings, wraths, strifes, backbitings, whisperings, swellings, tumults:

...lest there be debates, envyings, wraths, strifes, backbitings, whisperings, swellings, tumults: All these are products of carnal reasoning. None of them are physical, yet any one of them could, and too often, does generate physical reactions. Paul addressed this

very issue in his first Corinthian epistle in chapter 1, verses 10, 11: *Now I beseech you, brethren, by the name of our Lord Jesus Christ, that ye all speak the same thing, and that there be no divisions among you; but that ye be perfectly joined together in the same mind and in the same judgment.*

[11] For it hath been declared unto me of you, my brethren, by them which are of the house of Chloe, that there are contentions among you.

I shall not find you such as I would, and that I shall be found unto you such as ye would not: Can we not easily detect Paul's apprehension of their having greatly sinned, and the congregation's fear of his reprisals? That congregation had witnessed the signs and wonders that accompanied Paul's ministry. They feared his spiritual power.

21And lest, when I come again, my God will humble me among you, and that I shall bewail many which have sinned already, and have not repented of the uncleanness and fornication and lasciviousness which they have committed.

...my God will humble me among you: Paul rejoiced greatly when idolaters were won to God. To learn that some of those converts had reverted to their former natures, would have distressed and humbled him greatly. He would have been acutely reminded that he was no more than a mere man; he could win souls, but he could not keep all of them faithful to God.

...not repented of the uncleanness and fornication and lasciviousness which they have committed: It is rather shocking to think that any congregation would allow anyone guilty of the sins here mentioned to long remain as members of the congregation. Again, it seems that the false prophets in the Corinthian church had proselyted quite successfully.

...and that I shall bewail many... Many: Not 1 or 2, but many! Oh, pastor, let not the devil bow your soul to the ground every time a person turns his/her heart from God. When speaking of seed being sown, Jesus said that some would fall on stony ground, giving no

depth of earth for the seed to survive; some among thorns, which would kill the germinated seed; but some would fall on good ground and survive. Keep sowing, oh man of God, and trust God to guide your seed to good ground. Much of your seed will not survive, no matter how much you weep over lost souls. Keep sowing.

Bob Koonce Th. D.

CHAPTER THIRTEEN

1 This is the third time I am coming to you. In the mouth of two or three witnesses shall every word be established.

2 I told you before, and foretell you, as if I were present, the second time; and being absent now I write to them which heretofore have sinned, and to all other, that, if I come again, I will not spare:

3 Since ye seek a proof of Christ speaking in me, which to youward is not weak, but is mighty in you.

4 For though he was crucified through weakness, yet he liveth by the power of God. For we also are weak in him, but we shall live with him by the power of God toward you.

5 Examine yourselves, whether ye be in the faith; prove your own selves. Know ye not your own selves, how that Jesus Christ is in you, except ye be reprobates?

6 But I trust that ye shall know that we are not reprobates.

7 Now I pray to God that ye do no evil; not that we should appear approved, but that ye should do that which is honest, though we be as reprobates.

8 For we can do nothing against the truth, but for the truth.

9 For we are glad, when we are weak, and ye are strong: and this also we wish, even your perfection.

10 Therefore I write these things being absent, lest being present I should use sharpness, according to the power which the Lord hath given me to edification, and not to destruction.

11 Finally, brethren, farewell. Be perfect, be of good comfort, be of one mind, live in peace; and the God of love and peace shall be with you.

12 Greet one another with an holy kiss.

13 All the saints salute you.

14 The grace of the Lord Jesus Christ, and the love of God, and the communion of the Holy Ghost, be with you all. Amen.

I think it highly possible that Paul wrote many letters that have not been preserved. There is scriptural proof that at least 1 epistle did not survive. Colossians 4:16 reads: *And when this epistle is read among you, cause that it be read also in the church of the Laodiceans; and that ye likewise read the epistle from Laodicea.*

Ingesting food assuages hunger; Scripture reading increases hunger in a reader to read and learn more of the Word of God. A serious student of Scripture is never content with a once-over reading. Each session beckons a new one and whets an increasing hunger in the soul to know more about God, the Creator of all things; His manifestation in the person of Jesus Christ, and the promises He has given to all believers.

Chapter 13 closes another of Paul's extant letters to Corinth. I conscientiously cannot say that II Corinthians is Paul's second and final letter to the Corinthians. Paul founded many churches, separated by great distances to be traveled by foot, all in a period of time devoid of speedy transportation and communication. It would have been physically impossible for him to have ministered to every church for extended periods in order to address the needs of every church. He surely must have penned many letters of which we have no record.

1 This is the third time I am coming to you. In the mouth of two or three witnesses shall every word be established.

This is the third time I am coming to you: Please refer to the comments on II Cor. 12:14 for my explanation for this clause. I agree with the Jamieson-Faucett-Brown interpretation that "third time" describes a physical visit and not a determination to visit. However, I think that commentary errs in its description of third time. I am surprised that so many commentaries disagree on the words, *In the mouth of two or three witnesses.* Several commentaries supply several different opinions; none that I have consulted link the expression to 2 or 3 scriptural proofs.

Moses' Law established the decree for 2 or 3 witnesses to confirm truth:
Deut. 17:6: At the mouth of two witnesses, or three witnesses, shall he that is worthy of death be put to death; but at the mouth of one witness he shall not be put to death.

Deut. 19:15 One witness shall not rise up against a man for any iniquity, or for any sin, in any sin that he sinneth: at the mouth of two witnesses, or at the mouth of three witnesses, shall the matter be established.

Jesus confirmed the edict in Matthew 18:16:
Matthew 16 But if he will not hear thee, then take with thee one or two more, that in the mouth of two or three witnesses every word may be established.

In the first verse of this chapter, Paul wrote:
... In the mouth of two or three witnesses shall every word be established.

In II Peter 1:20, Peter affirmed all the above in the following words:
Knowing this first, that no prophecy of the scripture is of any private interpretation.

More than 1 witness is needed to establish truth most surely translates as "multiple Scriptures." Single words rarely express complete thoughts. Rarer still, single words may be used in Scripture to convey whole thoughts. Scripture confirms Scripture—always. More than 1 Scripture is needed to correctly understand what is intended.

In Proverbs 15:22, Solomon wrote: *Without counsel purposes are disappointed: but in the multitude of counsellors they are established.*

2 I told you before, and foretell you, as if I were present, the second time; and being absent now I write to them which heretofore have sinned, and to all other, that, if I come again, I will not spare:

...as if I were present, the second time... I believe this expression should be worded, *"as if I were present as I was the second time."* Both Clarke's and Barnes' Commentaries insist that Paul visited Corinth but twice. As I have previously written, I believe that more than 2 visits occurred. Though Clarke disagreed with that assumption, he provided an explanation contrary to his own in his commentary:

Clarke:

"I told you before, etc. - As Calmet maintains that Paul had already been twice at Corinth, it is well to hear his reasons: 'St. Paul came to Corinth the latter end of the year of our Lord 52, and remained there eighteen months, Acts 18:1, etc. He came there a second time in the year 55, but stayed only a short time, as he had to return speedily to Ephesus, 1Cor. 16:7; hence it is that St. Luke makes no mention of this second journey in the Acts. Finally, he determined to visit them a third time; as in effect he did about the year 57. Of his second voyage to Corinth, which is not mentioned in the Acts, he speaks expressly in this verse."

3 Since ye seek a proof of Christ speaking in me, which to you-ward is not weak, but is mighty in you.

The verse delivers the connotation of, *"The proof of Christ speaking in me is in how mightily my preaching affects you. You are the proof."*

"Since ye seek a proof of Christ - The conversion of the Corinthians was to themselves a solid proof that Christ spoke by the apostle; and therefore, he could, with great propriety, say that this power of Christ, far from being weak, was mighty among them." (Clarke)

Jamieson-Fasscet-Brown Commentary gives the following comment:
- "Since — The reason why he will not spare: Since ye challenge me to give a "proof" that Christ speaks in me. It would be better if ye would *"prove* your own selves" (2Cor. 13:5). This disproves the assertion of some that Scripture nowhere asserts the infallibility of its writers when writing it.
- "which — 'who' (Christ).
- "is not weak — in relation to you, by me and in this very Epistle, in exercising upon you strong discipline.

"mighty in you —--has given many proofs of His power in

miracles, and even in punishing offenders (2Cor. 5:11, 2Cor. 5:20, 2Cor. 5:21). Ye have no need to put me to the proof in this, as long-ago Christ has exhibited great proofs of His power by me among you (2Cor. 12:12) [Grotius]. It is therefore not me, but Christ, whom ye wrong: it is His patience that ye try in despising my admonitions, and derogating from my authority:"

4 For though he was crucified through weakness, yet he liveth by the power of God. For we also are weak in him, but we shall live with him by the power of God toward you.

Some older manuscripts omit "bold", making the sentence read: *For he was crucified.* I believe this is the whole sense intended by Paul. He was not delivering a message of, "He might have been crucified," but a truth that "He had been crucified."

...was crucified through weakness... And being found in fashion as a man, he humbled himself, and became obedient unto death, even the death of the cross (Philippians 2:8).

...he liveth by the power of God... And Jesus came and spake unto them, saying, All power is given unto me in heaven and in earth (Matthew 28:18).

...we shall live with him by the power of God: But if the Spirit of him that raised up Jesus from the dead dwell in you, he that raised up Christ from the dead shall also quicken your mortal bodies by his Spirit that dwelleth in you (Romans 8:11).

5 Examine yourselves, whether ye be in the faith; prove your own selves. Know ye not your own selves, how that Jesus Christ is in you, except ye be reprobates?

Examine yourselves: Up to this very point, Paul defended himself as being a true apostle. This expression zeroes all attention onto the Corinthians: *Examine yourselves...prove your own selves:* Paul's words leave the inference of, "You have searched for a fault in me, and found none.

Now it's time to examine yourselves and see if you can attest to the same fact of being faultless."

Know ye not your own selves? Jesus Christ is in you, except ye be reprobates. The oft-used expression, "This is where the men are separated from the boys," becomes applicable. Paul knew that they knew whether they did or did not possess the Spirit of Christ. He hesitated not at all in labeling the pretenders reprobates.

6 But I trust that ye shall know that we are not reprobates.

I trust (I hope)
...ye shall know... The true sense of this phrase depends upon an understanding of the results of the previous verse. "Examine yourselves," he wrote in that verse. If and when they followed that instruction, they would immediately have determined whether they were or were not truly converted. Being converted proved the effectiveness of Paul's preaching. He had ministered good into their lives. Being unconverted identified that person as a hypocrite. "Now," Paul's words insinuate, "you can see for yourselves that we do not behave as do the reprobates among you."

7 Now I pray to God that ye do no evil; not that we should appear approved, but that ye should do that which is honest, though we be as reprobates.

...not that we should appear approved: Paul was cognizant of so many evil things the people in the Corinthian church had previously committed. He appeared to always be apprehensive that they might revert to old sins or practice new ones. These words deliver the thought, "We are not seeking credit for your conversion and growth in Christ. I write only to admonish you to *do no evil...but that ye should do that which is honest.*"

...though we be as reprobates: The dissenters, false apostles among them, and the reprobates labeled Paul and his helpers reprobates. The phrase delivers the connotation, "Some among you label us reprobates, and even if you accept that as truth, I write that you not sin."

8 For we can do nothing against the truth, but for the truth.

Before I read submissions from several commentaries on a verse or passage of verses of Scripture, I stop to reason what message the passage delivers to me. Verse 8 is not a defense. Paul was not presenting the thought, "It would be futile to fight truth, so we surrender to it." Rather, the thought, "Truth prevails against every lie, and we are privileged and blessed to preach that truth." F.B. Meyer penned a profound statement on this verse: 'None can really injure the truth or stop its victorious progress. As well try to stop the sunrise.'"

9 For we are glad, when we are weak, and ye are strong: and this also we wish, even your perfection.

For we are glad, when we are weak can be understood as his saying, "When you think us weak in power and authority." Perhaps a more correct meaning for this clause would be: "When we are fatigued in our bodies and when our souls weary."

...we are glad... ye are strong... I understand this statement to say that the Apostle was sincerely happy when the Corinthians truly were strong. Conversely, the statement could be debated to mean that he rejoiced when they thought themselves strong. I think the second definition could be correct only in the sense that Paul's resolve to win them would have been strengthened, causing him to rejoice. The second definition is inconceivable in my mind.

10 Therefore I write these things being absent, lest being present I should use sharpness, according to the power which the Lord hath given me to edification, and not to destruction.

...being absent, lest being present... Distance between a shouter and they who hear the shout weakens the clarity of the shout. Paul used this sense in that statement. Being absent from them denied him the punitive power he possessed in the spirit to punish them as he would have done if present with them.

Sharpness-from the Greek αποτομια, meaning "a cutting off". The man, Paul, who wrote, *For I could wish that myself were accursed from Christ for my brethren, my kinsmen according to the flesh* (Romans 9:3), would never have acceded to the thought of permanently rejecting those he had labored so hard to win to God. The sharpness, the power given him by God, was for the edification and not for the destruction of the Corinthians, he contended.

11 Finally, brethren, farewell. Be perfect, be of good comfort, be of one mind, live in peace; and the God of love and peace shall be with you.

Finally—my last words to you, *brethren*—my kinsmen in Christ Jesus--I bid you *farewell*—such a lonely sounding word. No doubt that great apostle's heart travelled with that letter.

12 Greet one another with an holy kiss.
13 All the saints salute you.
14 The grace of the Lord Jesus Christ, and the love of God, and the communion of the Holy Ghost, be with you all. Amen.

Rather than proving the doctrine of the trinity of God, this verse does the opposite. Remove the conjunction "and" as it should be from the sentences, and the verse reads: *The grace of the Lord Jesus Christ, the love of God, the communion of the Holy Ghost, be with you all. Amen.* One God's grace demonstrated in three ways.

And may God bless you, my reader, for consulting this commentary as you studied God's wonderful Word!

Bob Koonce

Made in the USA
Columbia, SC
07 March 2020